EVERYDAY WEATHER
and how it works

revised edition

also by Herman Schneider
EVERYDAY MACHINES AND HOW THEY WORK
and with Nina Schneider
YOUR TELEPHONE AND HOW IT WORKS
SCIENCE FUN WITH MILK CARTONS

EVERYDAY
and

WHITTLESEY HOUSE   McGraw-Hill Book Company, Inc.

NEW YORK   LONDON   TORONTO

WEATHER
HOW IT WORKS

REVISED EDITION

by HERMAN SCHNEIDER

Lecturer in Science Education, City University of New York

pictures by JEANNE BENDICK

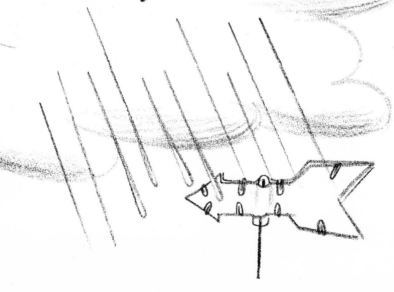

For my children,
who hold me responsible for the weather

With cordial thanks to Julius Schwartz, good friend and
meteorology instructor, for his critical reading of the
manuscript.

SECOND EDITION
Library of Congress Catalog Card Number: 61-12431

Published by Whittlesey House
A division of the McGraw-Hill Book Company, Inc.
Printed in the United States of America

Third Printing

CONTENTS

HOW DOES THE
WEATHERMAN KNOW?

CLOUDY AND RAIN FRIDAY, FAIR AND WARMER SATURDAY, says the weatherman. That's good news for you, because you've planned a trip to the country. Perhaps you feel a bit grateful to the weatherman, even though you know he didn't actually arrange the weather for you. And perhaps you wonder—how does he know what the weather will be tomorrow and the day after?

Predicting tomorrow's weather, and the weather for several days in advance, is no simple job of course. To do it accurately, the weatherman needs lots of instruments and charts, and years of training. But understanding today's weather is easier. You can find out without instruments or charts why a certain shape of cloud will bring thunder-showers in a very short time, while another shape tells you that you can plan an afternoon outdoors.

There are some things you know right now that can help you understand weather.

For example, you know that when you take a shower, the bathroom mirror will become cloudy. When you understand why, you will know how real clouds are formed. You know that the quickest way to "air" a room is to open the windows top and bottom. When you understand why, you will know what makes the wind blow.

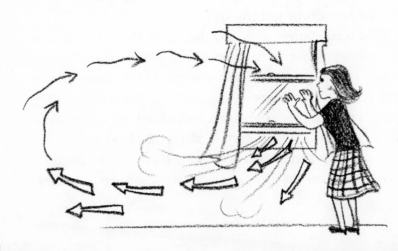

This book will help you to "understand why" about all kinds of weather—about calm days and windy days, about fog and rain, snow and sleet, lightning and thunder, hailstorms and tornadoes. There are simple experiments that will help you to find out for yourself, and there are directions for building your own weather bureau instruments out of materials you have in your house. If you build the instruments, and if you keep a daily record of what you find out with them, you will be able to try your own weather forecasting. You will make more wrong predictions than the weatherman, but you'll have lots of fun, and as you keep it up, you'll get better and better at it.

WHAT MAKES THE WEATHER?

RAINY, CLOUDY, SUNNY, BALMY, CLEAR, WINDY, HUMID, SNOW, HAIL, GALE, HURRICANE, TYPHOON, MONSOON, SLEET, TORNADO, CONDENSATION, EVAPORATION, PRECIPITATION. . . .

These are just a few of the words used to describe the weather. The weatherman knows many, many more. With such a long list of words to describe it, you might think that there must be a long list of things that go into making up the weather. Actually, there are only three:

And that's about all!

Every one of those weather words in that long list tells of some special thing that happens to heat, air, and water. In order to understand the causes of weather, let's find out more about these three great weather-makers. Let's begin with heat.

HEAT IN THE WEATHER

WHEN YOU WALK barefooted on a hot sandy beach, your feet feel hot. They feel that way because of the heat in the sand. Where did that heat come from? From the sun, of course. The sun gives all the heat for all the weather in the world. The weather is hot when lots of sunlight makes it so; the weather is cold when there is less sunlight.

But the weather isn't the same everywhere at the same time. It may be hot on the beach, but cool on the water. A winter day may be very cold even though the sun is shining brightly. A summer day in one part of this country may be much hotter than in another part. How can the same sunlight make different kinds of weather? To discover some of the answers, let's find out more about the heat that comes from sunlight.

HEAT PILES UP

If you leave a piece of dark paper in the sunlight for five minutes, it will feel hot to the touch. Put another dark paper next to it for only one minute, and you will find that it is only slightly warm. The more time in the sunlight, the warmer it gets. Heat piles up.

ABOUT 9 HOURS IN WINTER
AM   PM

ABOUT 15 HOURS IN SUMMER
AM   PM

Time in the sunlight is one reason why the weather is different at different times of the year. On a clear day in December, in the northern part of this country, the sun shines for about *nine* hours. Then, day by day, the sun rises a bit earlier and sets a bit later. Each day the sun shines a little while longer, until, when July comes around, there are about *fifteen* hours of sunlight each day. The more hours of sunlight there are, the warmer the weather. So July days are warmer than December days.

On a cloudy day, most of the sunlight is blocked off by the clouds. The earth is not warmed as much as it is on a clear day. So a cloudy day is usually cooler than a sunny day.

MORE SLANT, LESS HEAT

Now you know one reason why winter is colder than summer. There are fewer hours of sunlight. There's another reason, one that seems rather strange at first. Winter sunlight is cooler! It's the same sun, and it shines just as bright and hot as in the summertime, and yet the earth gets less heat from it.

How can the same sun give less heat at one time than another? Is it because we are closer to the sun in summer than we are in winter? Definitely not! In fact, the earth is actually a bit nearer to the sun during our winter, but not enough to make a difference one way or another.

The reason that winter sunlight is cooler is because the sun's rays come to us at much more of a slant than they do in summer. You may have noticed that the afternoon sun on a winter's day is low in the horizon. The summer sun, on the other hand, is much higher in the sky at the same time of day.

The direct rays from the overhead sun are much more concentrated than the rays which strike the earth at a slant. You can see this for yourself by experimenting with a flashlight. Hold the flashlight so that the beam shines straight down on a sheet of white paper. Notice the bright circle of light.

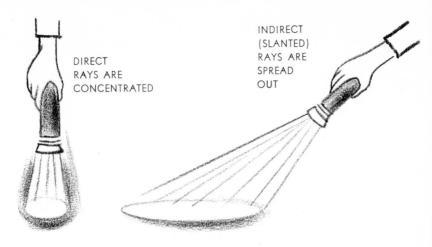

DIRECT RAYS ARE CONCENTRATED

INDIRECT (SLANTED) RAYS ARE SPREAD OUT

Now tilt the flashlight so that the beam strikes the paper at an angle. Do you see how the circle of light spreads out and becomes less bright?

So it is with sunlight. In winter, when sunlight comes to the earth at a slant, it gives less heat than in summer when it strikes the earth directly.

Another reason why slanted rays are weaker is that these rays must travel a longer distance through the air which surrounds the earth.

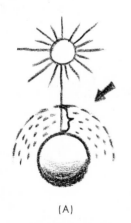

DIRECT RAYS TRAVEL A SHORTER DISTANCE (A) THROUGH THE ATMOSPHERE THAN SLANTED RAYS (B)

(A)

(B)

Direct rays coming straight down from overhead may travel through about 500 miles of atmosphere. Rays striking the earth at an angle have to plow through many more miles of gases, clouds, dust, smoke, and chemicals in the air. Thus these slanted rays lose more of their energy and give less heat when they reach the earth.

Winter and summer, the sun itself is the same, but the way it shines on the earth is different and therefore the amount of heat the earth receives is different. Winter is colder than summer for two reasons—there are fewer hours of sunlight per day, and the sun's rays are more slanting and therefore give less heat.

DARKNESS MAKES A DIFFERENCE

When you look at the earth from high up in an airplane, you can see that the earth's surface has many shades of light and dark. There are light-colored sandy beaches, dark fields and forests, and dark places where the earth has been freshly plowed. If there is snow on the ground, it shows lightest of all. Does darkness or lightness make a difference in the way the earth receives the sun's heat?

You can find out by placing two sheets of paper, one white and the other black, in the sunlight. The white paper will feel cool after five minutes, but the black will feel quite warm. White and light-colored things reflect light, that is, they let it bounce off. Black and dark-colored things absorb light, that is, they allow it to soak in and turn to heat.

WHITE THINGS
REFLECT LIGHT

DARK THINGS
ABSORB LIGHT

Darkness and lightness make a difference in the way things heat up. And this is one way that people can do something about the weather. In hot weather they may wear light-colored clothing to reflect the sunlight. In hot countries they may paint their houses in light colors.

Dark-colored places heat up more in the sunlight than lighter ones. And because the surface of the earth is dark in some places and light in others, the earth does not heat up evenly in the sunlight.

This also explains why spring weather comes later in snow-covered countries. The white snow, because it reflects the sunlight, remains cold and keeps the air cold. But in countries where snow does not fall during the winter, the dark earth can soak in the sunlight and warm up quickly. In such places the weather becomes warm sooner. On a sunny spring day the weather will be warmer where there are dark fields than where the soil is light-colored or covered with snow.

LAND AND WATER MAKE A DIFFERENCE

In the summer, people go to the beach to escape the heat of the city. It's cooler at the beach, even if you don't go into the water. You can find out why with a pair of soup plates.

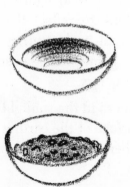

Half-fill one soup plate with cool water and the other with ordinary dry garden soil taken from a cool shady spot. Touch your fingertip to each, to feel how cool they are. (Better still, use a thermometer if you have one.) The temperature should be about the same.

SOIL GETS WARM,
WATER STAYS COOL

Place the two in sunlight for fifteen minutes. Then touch the surface of the soil and of the water. You will find that the soil feels quite warm, while the water remains fairly cool. In the sunlight, soil heats up faster than water.

The same is true of most materials. Sand, rock, wood, cement, brick—the materials of which a city's streets and houses are made, all heat up faster than water. And as they heat up, they make the air warmer. But the water in a lake or ocean stays cool, and it helps to keep the air cool too. That's why you're more comfortable at the beach on a hot day.

WHY LAND HEATS UP FASTER

Land heats up faster than water for several reasons. One reason is that water is always moving—up and down, back and forth, and from side to side. As the heat from the sun strikes the water's surface it is carried down deep by this constant movement. The heat which reaches the land, however, can't pass through easily to the part underneath. Have you ever noticed while you were digging in the soil or on a sandy beach that the surface was hot but it was quite cool a few inches down? This is because most of the heat of sunlight goes into heating just the surface of the land and little more.

When you hold a glassful of water up into the sunlight, you can see the sun shining right through. And sunlight that shines upon a lake or ocean does not stop at the surface. It keeps shining down through the water, gradually warming the water on its way down. This takes far longer than it does just to heat up a surface. This is another reason why the land heats up faster than water.

There is still another reason. Different kinds of substances need different amounts of heat to make them hot. Gold, iron, or copper, for example, need very little heat before they become warm. But it takes more heat to raise the temperature of water than it does for almost any other substance we know. And not only does water heat up more slowly than land but it cools off more slowly!

SUNLIGHT HEATS THE SURFACE

HOT HERE

COOL HERE

WATER FEELS WARM AT NIGHT

When you go bathing on a hot day, the water feels pleasantly cool, because it *is* cooler than the land. But if you have ever gone swimming at night, you have noticed that the water feels warmer. It isn't really warmer than it was in the daytime, but it feels that way. Your two soup plates can tell you why.

Take the two bowls, one with water and the other with dry soil, out of the sunlight and put them into the refrigerator. After fifteen minutes touch the surface of each. You will find that the soil feels quite cold, while the water feels just cool, barely cooler than when you took it out of the sunlight. Water cools off more slowly than soil or sand. Now let's see what that has to do with moonlight bathing.

THE WATER FEELS COOL BUT THE SOIL FEELS COLD

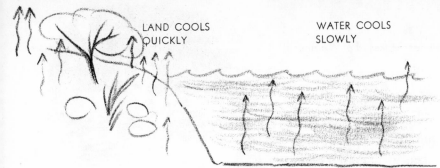

LAND COOLS QUICKLY   WATER COOLS SLOWLY

When the sun sets, the land, like the soil in the plate, cools off very quickly. Because only the surface was heated during the daytime, the heat can leave quickly. But the water cools slowly, because it was warmed through and through, not just at the surface. So at night the water feels warmer than the land, while in the daytime it's the other way around. Water heats up very little in the sunlight and cools off very little in the dark. Land heats up a great deal in the sunlight and cools off quickly in the dark.

NOT TOO COLD AND NOT TOO HOT

This difference between land and water is pleasant for swimmers. It means that you can enjoy a cool swim in the daytime, and yet not freeze if you go in at night. But it's much more important than that. It is the main reason why the weather can be so different in two places not very far apart. In the California desert, for example, it gets fiercely hot in the daytime and very cold at night, because the land heats up a lot and cools off a lot. But

not very far away, at the Pacific coast, the day isn't nearly as hot and the night isn't nearly as cold, because water heats up very little and cools off very little. The ocean water helps to even out the temperature of the air, both day and night. It helps to keep the nights from being too cold and the days from being too hot.

WARMER WINTERS, COOLER SUMMERS

Nearness to water has still another effect on the weather. It not only evens out the temperature between the day and the night, it evens out the seasons. Near water, the winters are not so cold nor the summers so hot, as inland places.

The water, heated by the sun all summer long, becomes warmer day after day. When winter comes, the water, still warm from the summertime, gives its heat slowly into the air. This helps to keep the air from cooling off rapidly. So winter weather is milder. The changes from summer to winter take place slowly in places near the ocean.

THE WATER IS STILL GIVING OFF HEAT IN THE WINTER

For example, Eastport, Maine, is near the Atlantic Ocean. The daytime temperature in January is just a little below freezing. The average is about 30 degrees. Bismarck, North Dakota, is just as far north, but is some distance away from any large bodies of water. The January temperature is about zero. Thirty degrees below freezing makes a big difference in the weather, and a big difference in the way you dress and feel.

When we look at the July temperatures, we find another interesting pair of numbers—Eastport, 70 degrees, Bismarck, 90 degrees. That is the difference between pleasant warmth and uncomfortable heat. At 70 degrees you can play tennis, hike, and be active and still comfortable. At 90 degrees it's easier only to think about sports and sit in the shade. Nearness to water gives Eastport the cooler summer weather.

The same sun shines on both cities, and the slant of the rays is the same. But Eastport's weather is kept moderate most of the year by the slow cooling and heating of the water, while Bismarck, far from the ocean, is hotter in summer and colder in winter.

SUN, THE WEATHER-MAKER

Now you see how the sun's heat is one of the great weather-makers of the world. Day after day, season after season, the sun shines steadily and evenly. But the sunlight, as it strikes the earth, gives its heat in different ways that make different kinds of weather.

MANY HOURS OF SUN
MAKE HOT WEATHER

When it shines for many hours each day, the heat piles up, and we have the hot weather of summer. When the hours of sunlight are few, the weather is cooler. The hours of sunlight make a difference in the weather.

The way the sun strikes the earth makes a difference in the weather, too. In summer, when the rays shine more directly against the earth, the sun's heat is more intense than in winter, when the rays are slanting and therefore cooler.

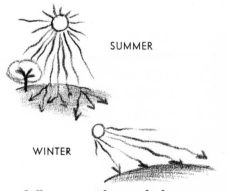

SUMMER

WINTER

The color of the earth makes a difference. The sunlight is soaked in by dark-colored things, so that they heat up quickly; but light-colored things reflect the sunlight and remain cool. At the same height a light-colored mountain slope would be cooler than a dark mountain would.

The heat of the sun makes different weather on land and on water. Land heats on the surface, and the air gets hot too. Water, because it allows the sunlight to shine through, heats up in a different way from land, and serves to even out the temperature of nearby places.

THE HEAT OF THE SUN MAKES DIFFERENT
WEATHER ON LAND AND WATER

But the weather is made by other things besides sunlight. Right now, if you're reading this in a room, away from the window, there is no way for the sunlight to reach you. Yet, when you open the window, the outside weather reaches you quickly enough, in the form of wind that blows into your room.

What made it blow in? The heat of the sun! Let's see how sunlight makes the wind blow.

HEAT AND AIR IN THE WEATHER

WHAT MAKES the wind blow, and what makes it stop? Why it is warmer above a hot radiator than underneath it? Why is it colder on top of a mountain than in the valley below?

These three questions seem to have nothing to do with each other. Yet all three are questions about the same thing—air. And when you know the answers, you will know a good deal about much of the world's weather. You can find the answers in a soda bottle and a balloon.

Snap a balloon over the neck of an empty soda bottle. The balloon will hang limp. Then place the bottle in a bowl of hot water and watch for results. You'll see the balloon rise and fill out, as if someone were blowing into it.

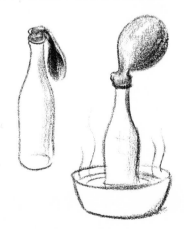

What happened? Did more air come into the bottle and balloon? Of course not; there is no opening for air to come in. But the balloon did fill out. There is more air in the balloon than when you started. That air came from the bottle. We say that the air in the bottle expanded—got bigger—when it was heated. As it expanded, it pushed its way up into the balloon. And if you take the bottle out of the hot water, allowing the air to cool off, you will see the balloon shrink as the air inside shrinks back to size.

Scientists have found out what goes on inside the balloon and bottle. This is the story.

The air is not one whole complete thing. It is made of many, many tiny separate things. These are called molecules.

The molecules of air are not close together, like marbles packed in a box. The molecules of air are flying around wildly, bumping each other and bouncing away, like a room filled with thousands of flying ping-pong balls.

But ping-pong balls don't just go bouncing around by themselves. Somebody has to keep slapping away at them to keep them moving. What keeps the molecules of air in motion? Why don't they slow down and fall to the bottom in a heap? The second part of our experiment tells the answer.

WARMER MEANS FASTER

When we place the bottle in the bowl of hot water, something happens to the molecules of air in the bottle. They begin to fly around more quickly and violently. When they bump into each other, they bounce away with greater speed than they did when the air was cooler. In warm air the molecules move quickly; in cool air they move more slowly. It seems that the speed of motion is somehow related to the heat.

And here is a strange fact—speed *is* heat! When we say, "The air is hotter today than yesterday," we could say it in another way too: "The air molecules are bouncing around more quickly today than yesterday." (But better not try it on your friends, or they'll begin to wonder if you've suffered a heat stroke.) And when we say, "I'd like a drink of cold water," we could just as well say, "I'd like a drink of slowly moving water molecules." "Hot and cold" can be said in another way—fast moving molecules and slow moving molecules.

MOLECULES OF COLD AIR

MOLECULES OF HOT AIR

31

Now we can understand what happened with the bottle and balloon. At first, when the air was cool, the molecules moved slowly. The molecules of cool air bounced against the wall of the balloon gently, without enough force to push out the sides. The balloon hung limply.

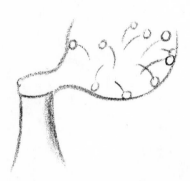

Then we heated the bottle and with it the air. When the air is heated, the molecules fly around more speedily. With greater speed they bounce harder and move farther apart from each other with each bounce. Now, when they strike the side of the balloon they strike harder and they push the sides out. The balloon rounds out. The difference between the motion of the molecules of hot and cold air is like the difference in force between a slow moving baseball and one that comes scorching into the catcher's mitt.

Now we know why air expands when it is heated— because the faster moving molecules bounce farther apart from each other. In the balloon and bottle there are the same total number of molecules, but they have pushed farther apart and so they take up more space.

A MOLECULE OF COLD
AIR MOVES THIS WAY

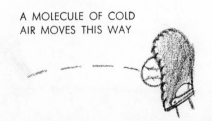

A MOLECULE OF HOT
AIR MOVES THIS WAY

20° COOLER INSIDE

We also know what the air molecules are doing on a hot day. They are bouncing more rapidly. And when you step out of a cool room into the hot street, you go from slowly moving molecules to rapidly moving molecules. The rapidly moving molecules bounce against your skin more violently and you feel hotter.

COLDER IS HEAVIER

If you could fill a quart bottle with air from a cool place and then go out on a hot street and fill another quart bottle with warm air, you would find something else. If you weighed the two bottles of air on a very accurate scale, you would find that the quart of cold air is heavier. (Of course the bottles themselves would have to be exactly alike in weight.)

The cold air is heavier because the slowly moving molecules are close together, so that more of them are crowded into the bottle. The faster moving molecules of warm air spread farther apart so fewer of them fit into the same sized bottle.

Cold air is heavier than warm air.

Here's a way to actually see for yourself that cold air is heavier. You will need two dry glass jars, pint size or larger. Drinking glasses will do too, but the effect is better with jars because they are larger. You will also need a sheet of paper larger than the mouth of the jar, and a friend ready to produce smoke by lighting the end of a piece of rope with a match. The smoke is needed to "darken" the cold air, so that you can see it moving.

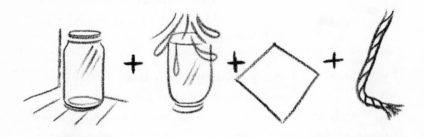

Put one jar in the refrigerator for two or three minutes, to cool the jar and the air inside. While you're waiting, set the second jar in the sink and heat it by allowing the hot water to run over the outside of it. This will heat the jar and the air inside.

Now take the cold jar out of the refrigerator and have your friend insert the smoking rope into this jar for about five or ten seconds. When he removes the rope, immediately clap the sheet of paper over the mouth of the cold jar. Then place the mouth of the hot jar down over the

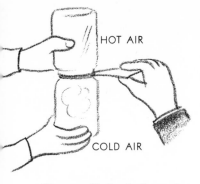

HOT AIR

COLD AIR

paper, exactly over the mouth of the cold jar. Hold the two jars steady while your friend slowly pulls the paper from in between the two jars. Now look at the smoke.

You will find that the smoke stays right where it is. The smoke, let's remember, is merely a way of making the cold air visible. So far, we find that the cold air, when it is underneath warm air, stays put. It looks as though cold air is heavier. Now let's make sure.

THE WARM AIR IS PUSHED UP

BY

THE HEAVIER COLD AIR

Keep holding the jars against each other, but now turn them upside down, with the cold air on top. You will see the smoke and cold air drop quickly into the lower jar. As the warm air is hit by the cold air, it is forced up into the top jar. Watch it whirl up. Now you can see that cold air is heavier than warm air.

WINDS IN YOUR ROOM

Now let's see what all this has to do with the weather. We'll begin with a small piece of it, the weather in your room early on a cold winter morning. The room is cold. All the air in your room is at about the same temperature.

In other words, all the molecules are moving at about the same low speed and are about the same distance apart from each other.

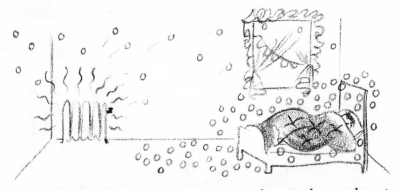

The radiator now begins to get hot. It heats the air right next to it. The warmed air molecules begin to move faster and bounce farther apart. Some of the molecules are pushed over to other parts of the room as the molecules in the warm air bounce faster and farther apart. There are fewer molecules now on the warmer side. Now the air is warmer and lighter on the radiator side of the room but still cold and heavy on the other side.

The cold air, which is heavier because it has more molecules crowded into it, pushes across the floor toward the part that has more space—the warmed, lighter air over the radiator. Here it is warmed, expands, becomes lighter, and rises. The cold air pushes the light warm air up and across the ceiling toward the opposite side. More cold air sinks down and moves across the floor toward the warmer side. More warm air rises. The hotter the radiator, the faster the air moves in this room-sized circle.

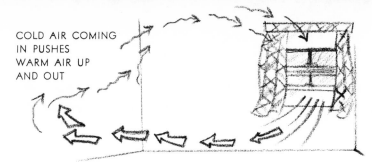

COLD AIR COMING
IN PUSHES
WARM AIR UP
AND OUT

This movement of warm and cold air—up, across, down, and back—is a small-sized wind. You use this same kind of air movement to freshen the air in a room. You open the windows top and bottom, allowing cool fresh air to come in through the bottom opening and push out the warm stale air through the top. This is a combination indoor and outdoor wind.

WINDS OUTSIDE

Real winds are large-sized movements of the air made in the same way. For example, at the seashore in the daytime the land is hot, like the hot radiator, while the water is cool like the cold part of your room. The cooled, heavier air rolls in from the water and pushes up the warmer, lighter air. This part of the air circle is the pleasant sea breeze. The rest of the circle brings the air up, across, and down to the water again. Over and over again the breeze blows in from the water as long as the sun's heat keeps the land hotter.

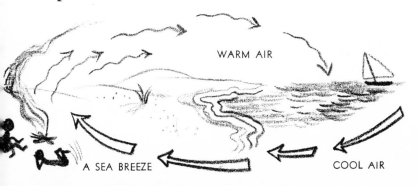

WARM AIR

A SEA BREEZE

COOL AIR

What happens at night? The sun sets, the land cools off until it is cooler than the water. You remember that land cools off much faster than water. The water at night is warmer than the land. Now the circle turns in the other direction. The warmer air over the water is pushed up by the cooler air rolling out from the land—a land breeze.

A LAND BREEZE

WINDS, BIG AND LITTLE

Everywhere in the world heat and air are at work, wheeling and whirling the air in circles of every size. Little winds drift gently from the cool shade of a tree, from the shady side of a street, from the cool water of a pond. Wind from the shaded side of a mountain sweeps down and across the sunny valley. Winds roll in from the ocean,

blowing across vast continents. From the huge icy wastes of the north the cold air flows across half the world, pushing aloft the warm air over jungles and deserts.

Where the warm air is just a little warmer than the cool air, the breeze is delicate, hardly enough to stir a leaf. Where the difference is greater, the circle of air turns faster and the winds blow stronger. The lightest breeze and the wildest gale, and all the winds that blow anywhere in the world, are made by the circling, swirling air.

As you can see, the sun is really the cause of winds. Without the sun, the air would not be heated, and part of the air must be heated to make it flow and circle around. Heat and air, working together, make the winds of the world.

ANOTHER HEATING SYSTEM

Let's look at another way in which the air is heated and see what this has to do with weather. Suppose you are in St. Louis and the temperature is an almost unbearable 105 degrees. How far would you have to travel to cool off? Five hundred miles north to Canada? Certainly not. You could find freezing weather only a few miles away provided you went straight up!

The air on the ground is quite different from the air up above. To understand why, we have to study the atmosphere—the air that surrounds us.

Think of the air above us as a soft, thick blanket that

covers the earth. Nobody knows exactly where the air ends because there is no sharp boundary between the atmosphere and outer space. But scientists have discovered different layers in our air blanket.

The lowest layer, called the troposphere, is the most interesting to the weatherman because here is where he finds the clouds, rain, snow, and storms that make up our everyday weather. The troposphere goes up only about 5 miles at the poles and a little more than 10 at the equator.

Beyond these limits we have another layer—the stratosphere. This layer is practically free of changes in the weather and is about 50 miles thick. Above the stratosphere lies the ionosphere which stretches out for about 500 miles into space.

Why should we be concerned with the outer layers of atmosphere if weather occurs only in the troposphere? There are several reasons. For one thing, scientists believe that someday the strange behavior of the weather will be better explained by studying the upper air.

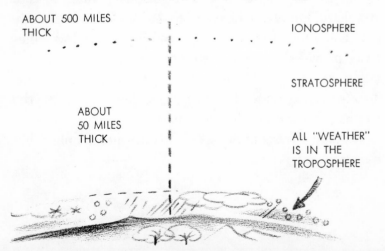

ABOUT 500 MILES THICK

IONOSPHERE

STRATOSPHERE

ABOUT 50 MILES THICK

ALL "WEATHER" IS IN THE TROPOSPHERE

For example, during World War II, pilots discovered a great stream of strong winds that flows from west to east in the upper troposphere. This is the jet stream which is shaped like a giant, curved tube more than 300 miles wide and about 4 miles high. In the center of this

great air current the winds may reach over 250 miles per hour. Toward the edges the wind is milder, somewhere between 50 and 100 miles an hour.

The pilot of a high-flying eastbound plane can latch on to the jet stream and use it as a tail wind. Thus many hours and precious fuel can be saved. Westbound pilots must avoid the jet stream entirely.

Recently it was discovered that as the path of the jet stream changes, weather changes occur on the earth. No doubt more knowledge of upper air currents such as the jet stream will help us predict the weather on the ground.

Still another reason for studying the upper atmosphere is this. In our space age many rockets and satellites will travel through the stratosphere and ionosphere. Before a man can be safely sent into space, we must find out as much as we can about what he can expect on his journey.

BACK TO EARTH

Let us get back to earth, or at least to the troposphere, to see why it should be freezing in the stratosphere while the ground is scorched in St. Louis down below. Why should it be so much colder up high? There are several ways to explain this.

Have you ever seen a pile-up of players at a football game? The man at the bottom often comes up bruised because of all the weight on top. Now think of the pile-up of air molecules in the atmosphere. Layer after layer of air presses down and the molecules near the bottom are squeezed closer together. It is easy to understand why the air closer to the earth becomes hotter than the air up above.

In the first place, the air molecules which have been squeezed are much closer together. This means they will bump into each other more often; they bounce and jiggle more quickly and violently and this results in more heat.

Secondly, the lower molecules are closer to the ground and they are more easily warmed as the sun's heat is reflected from the earth's surface. Also, since there are more molecules lower down, the total amount of heat absorbed is greater.

Finally, as warm air rises in the atmosphere, its molecules spread out as the air expands. This makes them lose some of their energy and the air cools off.

You can test this yourself very quickly. With your mouth wide open, gently blow your breath against the back of your hand. Does it feel warm? Now, with your

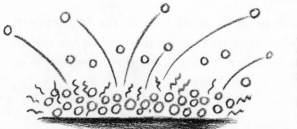

AS THE AIR MOLECULES RISE AND SPREAD OUT, THE AIR COOLS OFF

mouth almost closed, blow against the back of your hand. Your breath feels cool!

You forced air through a small opening, so that it spread out after it passed your lips. When air expands from a small space to a larger one, it becomes cooler.

Air at the top of a mountain is cooler than air at its base for the three reasons just given. This is why mountain tops even in hot countries like Mexico are covered with snow in the middle of the summer.

By its own weight, air helps make the weather. The air presses down on its lowest layers so that they are warmer than the air higher up. Valley air is hotter than mountain air.

As you see, air works for you in two ways. When it is moved by the sun's heat, it is the wind blowing across the land and the sea. When it is piled up, it compresses its lower layers and makes warmer weather. In both ways, air helps to make the weather you have where you live.

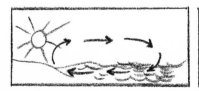 

WATER IN THE WEATHER

Rain, fog, snow, mist, clouds, hail, sleet, frost, dew. . . .

All these words tell something about water. All of them are water in the weather in one form or another. But what makes the difference in the forms? Why does water come down sometimes as rain and sometimes as snow or hail? And how did the water get up there in the first place?

HOW WATER CHANGES

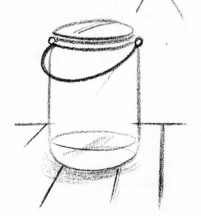

You can see part of the answer in a glass jar—a clean dry one. Into the jar carefully pour a small amount of water, about one-quarter inch deep (keeping the sides dry) and then put the cover on. Set the jar in the sunlight or in some moderately warm place. Let it stand for a half-hour or more. When you look at it again, you will see a misty film inside, on the side of the jar, and there may even be some large drops of water hanging down from under the cover.

How did the misty film and the water drops get up out of the bottom?

MOLECULES AGAIN

Molecules are the answer again, just as they were in air. Water, like everything else in the world, is made of separate tiny particles called molecules. These water molecules are not still, but keep bumping and jiggling around. They are much closer together than air molecules, and they don't move nearly so fast. But they never stop moving. As they jiggle and bounce around, those near the top bounce right out of the water. These molecules continue to go on their bouncing, jiggling way, but now they move around among the bouncing air molecules. We say these water molecules have evaporated into the air. Bit by bit, molecule by molecule, the water in the dish evaporates into the air. The water in the air is called water vapor.

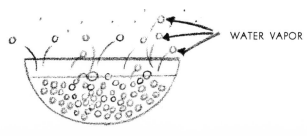

WATER VAPOR

COOLER AND SLOWER

Let's follow the molecules of water vapor. Bumping around in the air of the glass jar, some of the water molecules happen to be pushed over toward the side. When they touch the glass, some of them happen to be moving quickly and bounce back. But others may be moving a bit more slowly and they stick to the glass. Other water molecules bump into them and stick too. Soon the glass

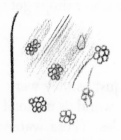

is covered with clusters of water molecules. Each cluster can be seen as a tiny drop of water. The many clusters together make the thin, moist film on the sides of the jar. We say that the water vapor has condensed on the sides of the jar.

EACH CLUSTER OF WATER
MOLECULES BECOMES A DROP

If we cool the sides of the jar, the molecules of water vapor move more slowly. More of them stick to the glass. We can say—water vapor condenses more quickly when it is cool.

Now let's see how these things that happened in a jar can help us to understand some facts about the weather.

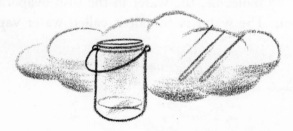

WATER IN ALL SHAPES AND SIZES

WATER EVAPORATES from the earth all the time. It evaporates from damp soil, from wet clothes on washlines, from puddles, from lakes and rivers and oceans. Water vapor is constantly being formed.

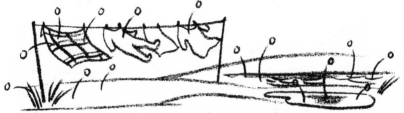

The water vapor stays in the air as long as it stays warm—that is, as long as the molecules move fast enough to keep bouncing away when they bump into each other.

When the water vapor is cooled, and the molecules move more slowly as they bump into each other, some of them stick together. When this happened in the jar, a film of tiny drops formed on the side. When this happens outside the jar, all kinds of things take place, depending on where the water vapor is, how much there is of it, and how much it is cooled. Let's look at a few examples.

DEW

At night, when the land cools off, it cools the water vapor in the air nearby. Then the water vapor condenses against anything cool. It forms a thin film of water on rocks and pebbles, on soil and plants. On the leaves of plants it cools into the little beads of water that we call dew. All night long the dew clings to the cool  things along the ground. In the morning, the sunlight makes the dewdrops sparkle with rainbow colors. Soon, as the sunlight warms the ground and the things on it, the dew evaporates into the air, invisible until the cool of the night comes once again.

FOG

Sometimes the air is thick with water vapor, almost too much for it to carry. When the air cools, the vapor begins to condense against anything cool. Some of the water vapor condenses on the dust particles and other specks in the air. Around each particle, a film of water forms as a tiny drop. Billions and billions of these drops swirling in the air form a fog that slows traffic to a crawl and starts the harbor foghorns hooting their warning. Then, when sun warms the land, the tiny drops evaporate once more into invisible water vapor and the air is clear again.

SMOG—MAN-MADE FOG

In some industrial cities there are other things in the atmosphere besides ordinary dust. Chemical fumes, smoke from factory chimneys and incinerators, and exhaust gases from automobiles constantly pollute the air. In such places, water vapor often condenses on these poisonous particles to form a smoky fog or smog. This may hang on for days while people develop smarting eyes, serious coughs, and sometimes even fatal lung diseases. Scientists are busily at work trying to solve the smog problem. Watch your newspaper to see what progress is being made.

CLOUDS

Sometimes the water vapor is carried higher up by rising air. When the water vapor cools up there, it condenses on grains of dust in the same way as fog. Such a high-up fog is called a cloud.

On a clear day, when you look up at what was a cloudless sky, you may see a cloud that wasn't there a few minutes earlier. It almost seems to have sneaked up on you. How did it get there? You can find the answer in a clean, dry milk bottle with its little cardboard top.

IN A WARM
PLACE THE
FOG DISAPPEARS

IN A COOL
PLACE IT
COMES
BACK

Blow gently into the bottle several times, until you see a film of water form along the sides. Then cover the bottle and put it in a warm place. You will see the film of water disappear. Warmth has caused the water to evaporate into the air in the bottle. But the water is still there, as you can easily prove for yourself. Just put the bottle (still covered) in a cool place, and you will see the water vapor condense into a film of water once again.

That's how clouds "sneak up" on you. The air up above may be full of molecules of water vapor, and yet be warm enough for the molecules to keep bouncing around. These separate molecules are too tiny to be seen, so the sky looks clear. Then the air and the water vapor cool off a bit. The molecules move more slowly and begin to stick to dust particles. Very soon they have collected into little clusters that you can see, and all the clusters together form a cloud.

In the same way that clouds suddenly appear without having come from somewhere, they can also disappear without going anywhere. A bit of heat does the trick. The heat may come from the chimneys of a city, from the sunny side of a hill, from a hot dry desert, from all sorts of places. It warms the cloud, scattering the clusters of water drops into separate water molecules again, too small to be seen. The cloud disappears, although all the water is still there.

CLOUDS ARE SIGNPOSTS

Can you imagine a ship-wrecked sailor, drifting along in an open boat, shouting with joy because he sees a cloud? If he does, it's because he knows that clouds are often signposts of land. The land may be just a small island, too low to be seen from far off. But high above it there will often be a ring of clouds that can be seen far away.

51

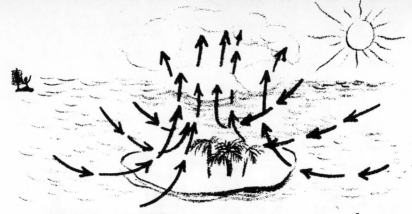

The ring of clouds is caused by heat, air, and water working together. The sun's heat has made the land hot so that the warm light air over the land is pushed up by cooler air blowing in from the ocean. This ocean air is full of water vapor, picked up from the spray on the waves. The water vapor is carried in over the land and then lifted up by the rising warm air. As it rises it meets cooler and cooler air. Finally the water vapor has cooled off enough to cling to dust particles and form a cloud that says "land ho!" to the sailor.

ALL KINDS OF DUST

Perhaps you are wondering about dust—how a cloud can possibly form in the clean fresh country air, or far out in the ocean, thousands of miles from cities. But dust is everywhere around the world, and it contains many different things. Over a city the dust may be smoke and grime particles, while out in the country it may be tiny pollen grains, fine powdery soil, and rock dust. Over the ocean there may be both kinds of particles blown out from the land, as well as dust and smoke particles from volcanoes and tiny crystals of salt from the ocean. But everywhere there are bits of dust in the air on which the water vapor can condense and form into fog near the earth or into clouds higher up.

RAIN

A cloud is an enormous number of tiny water drops. Each one of these water drops is a cluster of water molecules. These clusters are whirling and darting about in the air. When a cloud is cooled, the clusters move more slowly. When  they touch, they stick together and form larger and heavier clusters. Soon they are too heavy to stay up in the air, and they fall to the ground as rain.

RAIN-MAKING

Clouds in the air, no matter how big and full of water vapor, don't help the farmer whose fields need rain, or the city people whose reservoirs are running low. To be of use, the clouds must be-  come rain. Scientists think that clouds can be encouraged to turn into rain if we provide them with more particles around which the rain drops can form.

All kinds of particles have been tried for artificial rain-making. One kind that seems to work is a chemical called silver iodide. Tiny particles of this chemical can be scattered from an airplane. They can spread very well among the particles of water vapor, so that only a small amount of this harmless chemical can help a large cloud to form rain drops.

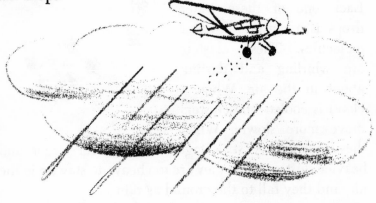

Another thing that seems to work is dry ice. Clouds can be cooled and possibly "dusted" by scattering bits of these crystals from a plane. The dry ice breaks up into tiny cold crystals around which water vapor can cool and condense.

Of course, artificial rain-making won't work on every cloud. It seems to work only on clouds that need a little push, that are *almost* cool enough or that have *almost* enough dust. But further experiments are being tried all the time, and some day we may be able to help ourselves to rainfall from any cloud, whenever we need it.

SLEET

Let's get back to ordinary rain, the old-fashioned kind that falls without the help of airplanes. Usually rain keeps falling until it reaches the ground. Sometimes, however, the raindrops fall through very cold air. Then the drops freeze into little bits of ice, called sleet. Sleet is frozen rain.

HAIL

Sometimes raindrops are picked up by a strong up-blowing wind, long before they reach the ground. They are flung high up where the air is cold enough to freeze them into drops of ice. When they fall, more water condenses around each ice drop. They are blown up again, so that in the icy cold upper air a new layer of ice freezes around the old. They fall toward the warmer air, pick up another layer of water, and are again blown upward to freeze still another layer of ice around the last. Again and again they fall and are blown upward. Again and again a new layer of ice is added. Finally, when they are too heavy for the up-blowing wind, they clatter to the ground as hail.

THE TRAVELS OF A HAILSTONE

When hail is falling, you can find out how many round trips the hailstones made before they fell to the ground. Get some hailstones. (Cover your head so you don't get hit!) After you have collected a few, bring them into the kitchen and set them down on a newspaper in the sink. Split one open. What you see inside will look like an onion. Count the rings, and you will know how many trips the hailstone made before it became too heavy for the up-blowing wind. Cut a few of the others and see if they all made the same number of trips.

IT WILL LOOK LIKE
THIS INSIDE

As you can guess, the stronger the upwind, the heavier the hailstones can grow. Fortunately the upwinds are usually not strong enough to lift the ice drops more than several times, so the hailstones fall when they are still too small to do much damage. But there have been hailstones bigger than tennis balls, that have smashed windows and destroyed crops, dented car roofs and even killed sheep grazing in fields. To build up such large hailstones, the upwind has to be a powerful 200 miles an hour.

SNOW

Sometimes the water vapor in the clouds is cooled so much that instead of collecting into raindrops it freezes into snowflakes. Snowflakes are not formed like sleet or hail. They are formed *directly* out of the water vapor in a cloud, while sleet or hail are formed from large clusters of water vapor which *first* were raindrops and then froze.

You can see the difference between snow and ice in your refrigerator. In the ice tray you have pieces of ice, which are really chunks of

SNOWFLAKES ARE FORMED DIRECTLY

SLEET AND HAIL WERE RAINDROPS FIRST

THIS FROST
IS LIKE SNOW

frozen water. These are like raindrops that freeze into sleet or hail. But around the ice tray compartment there is a white frost, which is really a kind of indoor snow. These white gleaming crystals were made directly from the water vapor in the air of the refrigerator. This water vapor did not first condense into water, and then become frozen. It changed directly from invisible water into six-pointed star-shaped crystals, like snowflakes that fall from the clouds.

As you can see, water vapor has many ways of coming back to the earth. When it is cooled slightly it forms the dew on the ground, or it changes to fog that hangs misty over the roads and rivers. Higher up in the sky it forms clouds. When these clouds are cooled, the water comes down as raindrops. If the raindrops are cooled still more on their way down, they reach the earth as sleet or hail. Or the water vapor may freeze directly into snowflakes, if the air is cold enough.

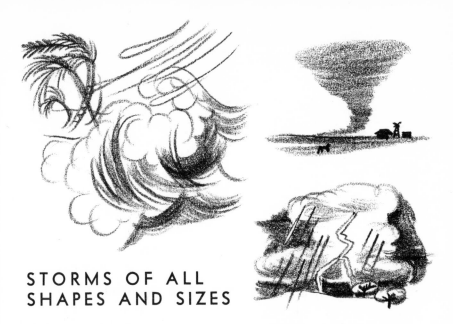

STORMS OF ALL
SHAPES AND SIZES

THE AIR AROUND you is never quite still. Even when you say, "There isn't a breath of air stirring," the air is moving, but not fast enough to suit you. When the air moves fast enough for you to feel it, you may call it a draft, especially if it's indoors, or a breeze. When it blows still faster, or stirs up some special kind of fuss, we have all kinds of storm names for it. Let's look at a few special kinds of storms, to see how they got that way.

MONSOONS

Monsoon is the Arabic word for season, and that's the kind of special storm it is—one that lasts a whole season. It is a wind that blows steadily for almost six months. Big monsoons blow across India and southern Asia, and smaller ones occur in Africa and parts of North and South America. Now we'll take a closer look at one.

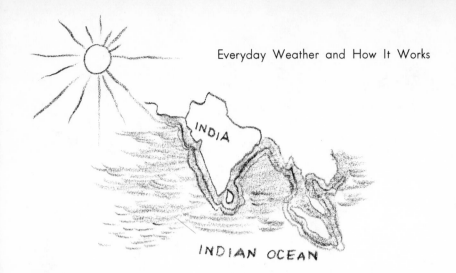

INDIAN OCEAN

India is near the equator. In the summer it receives lots of sunlight, direct and fierce, so that the land becomes very hot, much hotter than the Indian Ocean nearby. Soon the "wheel of air" begins to turn. That is, warm air over the land is pushed up by cooler air sweeping in from the sea. Up, out to the sea, down, and back to the land, the air keeps circling steadily for six months. But it isn't just a wind. Other things happen as well.

As the wind sweeps in from the ocean, it brings along huge quantities of water vapor picked up from the ocean. The water vapor is carried up by the rising warm air until it cools higher up and forms clouds. So far, nothing very special. This situation ought to give India some cloudy weather and occasional rains. But something else changes the situation quite a lot.

India is a gradually sloping land. It is low along the coast, but becomes higher inland and at the border near Tibet. The monsoons, blowing in from the sea, are lifted by the sloping land, higher and higher, much higher than if they had just risen as warm air. And the higher they go, the less squeeze on top, and the colder the air. This

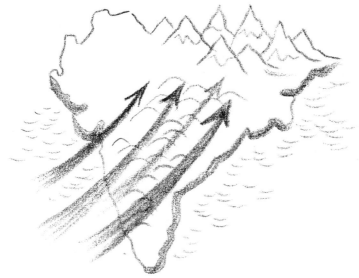

colder air causes practically all of the water vapor to be cooled into rain that falls on the land. The air, with its load of water vapor wrung out, then circles out to sea and down, to pick up a fresh load of water vapor for the next round trip. Over and over again, month after month, the land is drenched by the continuously circling wind, the summer monsoon. For this reason some parts of India have more rainfall than any other place on earth.

Other countries have their monsoons too, though the names may be different. In each case, summer is the time of inblowing winds and great amounts of rainfall—the

rainy season. And this is followed by the winter monsoon, when the land is cooler than the water, so that air blows away from the land toward the sea. With no water to pick up on the way, the wind is dry—the dry season. In most tropical countries, there are no summers and winters as we know them, just rainy seasons and dry seasons.

TORNADOES

Unless you live in the central part of the United States, you probably have never seen a tornado, but you should have no regrets at having missed the experience. These fierce, funnel-shaped windstorms can cause terrific damage. They can turn a big house into a pile of lumber in a few seconds, or can lift it up and whirl it around as if it were a sheet of newspaper. Fortunately, tornadoes are

rather narrow, so that they do their damage along a narrow track and then die out. The way they get started is quite interesting. We can find part of the answer by looking at your room.

In your room you probably have a radiator at one side. When the radiator gets hot, the air begins to circulate. That is, the warm air near the radiator expands and becomes lighter, so that the cool, heavier air at the other side of the room is able to sweep across the floor and push the warm air toward the ceiling.

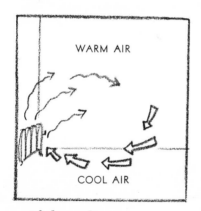
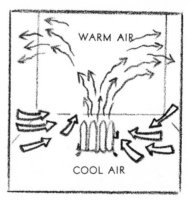

If the radiator were moved to the middle of the room, the circulation of air would be a little different. You would have a column of warm air in the middle of the room. It would rise toward the ceiling and spread out like an open umbrella, pushed up by cool air coming in from all sides toward the radiator. The cooler air would sweep in from every side toward the radiator and the warm column would rise quickly in the center.

The air circulating through the room moves because the heavy cool air pushes the warm air. How fast the air moves depends on the difference in temperature between the cool and warm air. When the difference is slight, the air moves slowly; when the difference is great, the air moves quickly. If the radiator were very hot, and the walls very cold, the movement would be very rapid. Then something new would happen to the column of upward-moving air above the radiator—it would begin to swirl around and around as it moves up. That swirling, upward-moving column of air is a miniature tornado.

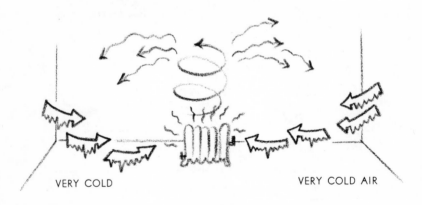

VERY COLD   VERY COLD AIR

You have seen such miniature tornadoes over a hot pavement near a shady wall, swirling the dust and scraps of paper around and around, and higher and higher.

Cool air from near the shady wall flows along the ground toward the hot pavement, pushing up the heated air in a little tornado.

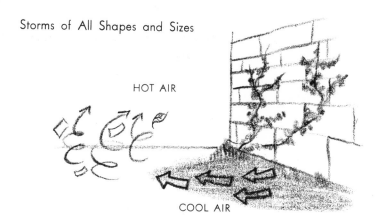

HOT AIR

COOL AIR

Big tornadoes are made in somewhat the same way, but on a much larger scale. In place of the hot pavement, there are miles and miles of hot prairie land, heating the air directly above it. In place of cool air from a shady wall, there is a large mass of cold air sweeping in from colder land farther north. Because the difference in temperature between the two airs is great, the movement of air is very rapid, and the upward moving warm air begins to whirl at a terrific speed. A tornado has begun.

As the heavy, cooler air keeps hurtling in, it brings dust, pebbles, water, bits of lumber and whole planks, horrified chickens and assorted small animals, and whirls them upward in the dark gray, dust-filled tornado, to be blown high up

HOT AIR

COOL AIR

and then dropped down hours later, miles away. The tornado travels along as it whirls, smashing and destroying until finally all the heated air that was next to the land has been squeezed high up by the cooler, inflowing heavy air. When there is no more warm air to be pushed up, the air stops flowing and the tornado is over.

HURRICANES

While a tornado can do great damage, it does it along a narrow track; you can be a half-mile away from the whirling spout and get nothing worse than a bad scare. But a hurricane covers a big area, and can really deliver a lot of punishment to anything standing in the way. Hurricanes have other names in other parts of the world

—typhoons, willy-willies, baguios, and cyclones—but they are all the same. All of them are huge whirling windstorms of enormous speed rushing in and pushing up a column of warm air. They are accompanied by vast quantities of drenching rain. They almost always occur in summer or fall. Let's look at one getting started.

A hurricane begins over water, in a vast calm stretch of ocean near the equator. The water is warmed by the sun, and so is the air right above it, day after day all summer long. Because this particular piece of ocean is far from land, there are no land-to-sea breezes to stir up the air. In the dead calm, the air above the water continues to become warmer and warmer. Then, from cooler places as with the tornado, cold air begins to stream in, and the hurricane is born. The warm air funnels inward

DAY AFTER DAY THE
SUN WARMS THE WATER
AND THE AIR AROUND IT

and upward in a spinning spiral that carries the warm moist air high up above the sea. There, where it is cooler, the water vapor condenses and comes down as a smash-

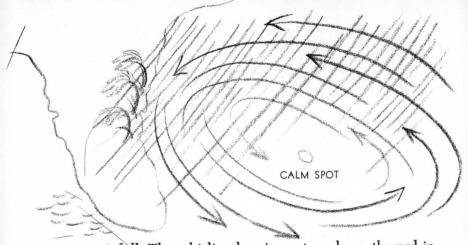

CALM SPOT

ing rainfall. The whirling hurricane travels northward in a great curved path, bringing furious winds and floods, blowing the sea into huge waves that sweep over beaches and nearby towns.

TORNADOES ARE SMALLER
AND BEGIN OVER LAND

HURRICANES ARE
HUNDREDS OF MILES
WIDE AND BEGIN OVER WATER

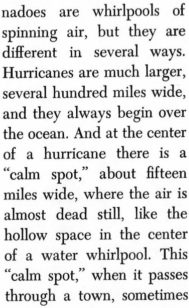

FLORIDA

Both hurricanes and tornadoes are whirlpools of spinning air, but they are different in several ways. Hurricanes are much larger, several hundred miles wide, and they always begin over the ocean. And at the center of a hurricane there is a "calm spot," about fifteen miles wide, where the air is almost dead still, like the hollow space in the center of a water whirlpool. This "calm spot," when it passes through a town, sometimes fools people into thinking that the hurricane is over; actually it is only half over, as the people soon find out when the spot has passed and the savage, drenching storm begins again.

THUNDERSTORMS

This kind of storm is not so huge and terrifying a spectacle as a hurricane, but on the other hand it is quite a show itself, complete with built-in lighting and sound effects—lightning and thunder. You can usually tell when a thunderstorm is heading your way by two special signs:

1. The shape of the cloud. A thundercloud is high and billowy, flat along the bottom and shaped somewhat like an anvil at the top.

2. The winds that come before it. First there is a gust of wind from where you

stand toward the cloud. Then it dies down, and another gust of wind springs up in the other direction, from the cloud toward you. Then it's time to put up your umbrella or run for shelter.

An airplane pilot once flew his plane into a thundercloud, to see what it was like. Several minutes later he came whirling out, upside down, his plane almost broken to pieces. A thundercloud looks quiet and fleecy from the outside, but inside it is a whirling, seething, violent mass of air, water vapor, rain, and even snow and hail. It's no fit place for man or beast—or airplane.

A thundercloud is formed by warm moist air that rises from the ground, cools into a cloud, and keeps piling up higher and higher. Finally it builds up to such a height that it reaches very cold air. The water vapor at this height condenses into rain, snow, or hail, that falls down

COOLER

WARMER

through the cloud. As it falls, it cools the inside of the cloud and sets up the whirling air currents that tumbled the airplane head over heels or rather nose over tail. The two winds that mark the coming of the thunderstorm are, first, the warm moist air rushing up to the cloud and, second, the cool air caused by the rain falling inside the cloud. This cool air, being heavier, falls down from the cloud and flows forward to fill the place of the rising warm moist air that caused wind number one.

LIGHTNING AND THUNDER

The exact cause of lightning in the sky is not entirely known but there is a kind of miniature lightning that you have made yourself, and that may partly explain the full-sized flashes. When you scuff your feet on a woolen carpet and then hold your finger near a metal door-knob, a little flash of electricity jumps between your fingers and the knob. Let's see why this happens.

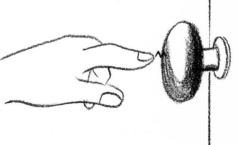

Everything, everywhere in the world, contains tiny particles of electricity. These particles are of two kinds, called electrons and protons. Ordinarily each thing contains an equal number of protons and electrons, unless

USUALLY EVERYTHING
HAS AN EQUAL NUMBER
OF PROTONS AND
ELECTRONS

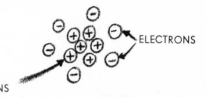

ELECTRONS

PROTONS

something special happens. One case of something special is the shuffling of your feet on the carpet. You scrape a pile of electrons from the carpet onto your shoes, and from there they spread over your clothes. But they aren't satisfied to stay by themselves; electrons never are, they want to team up with protons. When you hold your

finger near the metal door-knob, some of the electrons jump over, because electrons flow easily through metal. From there they drift farther, into the air and back to the carpet and the awaiting protons.

There are no carpets or shuffling feet in a thundercloud, but something like that probably happens, according to scientists. The rapidly whirling currents of air and rain inside the cloud cause a rubbing and tearing of the

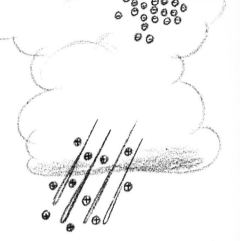

water drops, like the scuffing of your shoes against the carpet. This causes many electrons to be torn away and carried high up to the top of the cloud, while their proton partners are carried down by the falling raindrops. When this has gone on for some time, enormous quantities of electrons have piled up. Then in a split second they streak thousands of feet to another part of the cloud, to another cloud, or to the earth—wherever there happens to be a huge pile of protons in need of electron partners. As the electrons jump through the air, they cause the air to glow, and that glow is the flash of lightning.

Lightning is exciting to watch, but it is also very useful. Air contains great quantities of a gas called nitrogen. Plants cannot grow without nitrogen, but most plants have no way of taking it out of the air. Lightning causes nitrogen to be changed in such a way that it is absorbed by the water in raindrops. So rain that falls during a thunderstorm brings nitrogen into the soil, and the plants soak it up through their roots.

Thunder is really the sound effect of lightning. The electrons whizzing through set the air molecules dancing and jiggling faster. In that way the air is heated. This heating causes the air to expand suddenly and violently, and this expansion produces the crackling and rumbling sounds of thunder. Sometimes a lightning flash, that takes only a fraction of a second, may start a roll of thunder that goes on ten seconds or longer. This is the sound of the first clap of thunder, echoing and re-echoing back and forth among the hills and housetops.

You can tell how far away the lightning is by counting the time between the flash and the thunder. Count like this: one chimpanzee, two chimpanzees, three chimpanzees, etc. It takes about one second to count each chimpanzee. Divide the number of seconds by five and you will know the distance from the lightning flash to you, in miles.

Actually the flash and the thunder begin at the same instant, but light travels much faster than sound and reaches you sooner. Light travels about 186,000 miles per second, and sound about one-fifth of a mile per second. That's why you divide the chimpanzees by five.

The chance of your being struck by lightning is very, very, very small, much smaller than the chance of sitting down next to somebody in the bus and discovering that he has exactly the same name as you. However, even a tiny chance is something to think about, so if you're out in the open and lightning starts to zip around, keep these rules in mind:

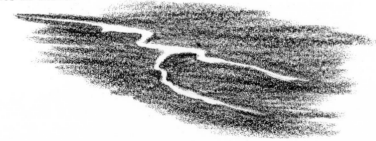

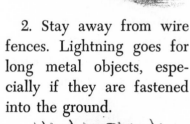

1. Stay away from under tall trees standing alone. Lightning flashes, when they strike, usually strike the highest thing around.

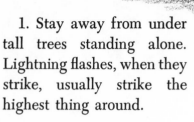

2. Stay away from wire fences. Lightning goes for long metal objects, especially if they are fastened into the ground.

3. If there is a house near-by, run to it—not to avoid lightning, but to stay dry.

4. If you can't get to a house, stay in an open field and take a soaking. It's safer than standing under a high tree or other high objects.

Lightning, thunder, thunderstorms, hurricanes, tornadoes, monsoons—there's lots of lively weather in the world, and let's be glad of it. These violent, showery, blowy things may be destructive at times, but most of the time they are very useful indeed, because they help to circulate the air and water vapor, to bring rain to the farms and fields, to bring nitrogen down to plants, to wash down the soot and smoke of cities. More often than not, storms are friends, not enemies.

YOUR WEATHER IS DIFFERENT

WHEN YOU MAKE plans several weeks ahead for a hike or a boat ride, you usually say or think to yourself, "weather permitting." Nobody can be very sure about the weather in this country several weeks ahead, not even the chief of the Weather Bureau. If the date is for some time in June, you can be fairly sure that the day will be warmer than a day in January. Whether it will be warm or hot, whether it will be clear, cloudy, or rainy, is anybody's guess.

But there are many places in the world where you could plan that boat ride a year in advance! For a certain date in June, for example, you could look up a table of figures that would give you the probable temperature and moisture of the air, and the probable amount of rainfall. And those figures would have a 20 to 1 chance of being correct. Where are these places in which the weather runs almost like clockwork?

NEAR THE EQUATOR AND NEAR
THE POLES THE WEATHER IS
LIKE CLOCKWORK

You can find clockwork weather in two kinds of places —in the hot countries near the equator and the cold countries near the North and South Poles. But in between, in the temperate zone, the weatherman has trouble predicting the weather even a week ahead. Why do the temperate zones behave that way?

This question puzzled the weather scientists (meteorologists) for a long time. In the last twenty years, however, most of the mystery has been cleared up, thanks to the patient work of many meteorologists. They in turn give credit to two important scientific achievements—the high-altitude airplane and the radiosonde.

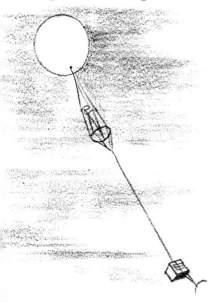

A radiosonde is a gasfilled balloon with a box attached, about the size of a large candy box. When the radiosonde is released, it floats up through the air to a height of ten miles or more. Inside is a little "weather bureau" that takes measurements of the temperature, moisture, and pressure of the air on the way up, and a tiny "radio station" that sends this information, in dot-and-dash code, to a receiving station on the ground. The radiosonde and the high-altitude airplane have enabled meteorologists to learn a great deal about the air high up, to add to what they already knew about the air closer to the ground.

Before going any further, you may as well set your mind at rest about what finally happens to that radiosonde drifting along in the air, miles high. After a while

the balloon bursts, as balloons will, and a little parachute opens up, allowing the box to drift slowly down to the ground. If you should find one of these boxes, you will see printed on it a request to drop it into the nearest parcel-post box, with the promise of a reward from the U.S. government if you do. The reward is money—anywhere from one to twenty dollars, depending on a code number on the box.

Now let's get back to The Mystery of the Temperate Zone, or Why Our Weather Misbehaves.

The answer is not a simple one. In fact, several chapters will be needed for the answer. But as you learn it, you will learn a great deal more about the weather, particularly about *how and why it changes*. You will get a bird's-eye view of the weather, so to speak, instead of the view from the ground that most people have. The answer has an impressive sounding title—Air Mass Analysis. Now let's find out what an air mass is, and how it is analyzed, and how the information is useful to us.

WHAT IS AN AIR MASS?

Air masses come in all sizes. The ones that make our weather are over 700 miles across. That's much too big to look at right now, when we're just getting started, so let's look at a little one first. We can find it in your refrigerator when you open it in the morning.

The air in that refrigerator is just air from the kitchen, not special air that came with the machine. Yet it feels and smells quite different from kitchen air. It feels colder and more moist, and it has the smell of various fruits, vegetables, and other foods in it. All those differences came about because the air mass *stayed quiet* for some time. During that time the air was chilled by the freezer coils, was made moist by water vapor from the damp vegetables, and was given its food smells by all the foods that had any smell to give. When air stands still for some time, it becomes changed by its surroundings.

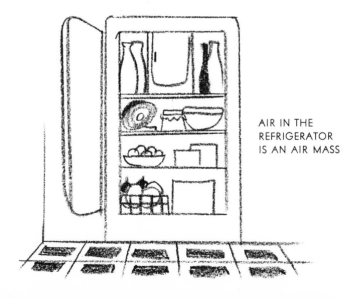

AIR IN THE
REFRIGERATOR
IS AN AIR MASS

The same thing happens outdoors in many parts of the world. There are no refrigerators, of course, but there are certain places in the world where the air stays quiet for long periods of time. Gradually the mass of air becomes changed by its surroundings, and after a while it moves on (we'll find out why later) and brings all kinds of interesting weather to the places over which it flows. Let's look at a sample.

Canada is an important weather-maker for most of the United States. Through most of the winter, the air there lies still, protected by the Rocky Mountains on the west.

THIS AIR IS THIN
AND COLD

THIS AIR BECOMES
COLDER
COLDER

The air near the snow-cov-ered ground becomes colder and colder, while the upper air is thin and cold to begin with. After days or weeks of lying quiet, the mass of air has become quite cold—and dry. It is dry because snow does not evaporate easily, and because cold air does not pick up water vapor quickly. (You know this be-cause you know wet clothes dry more slowly on a cold day.) We now have a vast, cold dry mass of air, and we call it a Polar Continental Air Mass. Now let's watch it go into action.

POLAR CONTINENTAL AIR MASS

The air mass, that has become colder, drier, and heavier all the time, pushes its way out and surges toward the south, into the United States. As it sweeps along, it brings a cold wave that chills half the country and may even reach as far south as Texas and Florida. But it isn't merely a cold wave, with everybody putting on warmer socks and buttoning overcoats. It's a cold wave with special attachments for different kinds of places. Here are two examples:

COLD AIR SWEEPS
DOWN SOUTH

1. As the Polar Continental Air Mass sweeps south, it rolls over land that is warmer than Canadian land. Winter sunlight in Canada is more slanting, and shines for fewer hours per day than in the United States, so Canadian land is colder. The warmer land of the United States causes the lower layers of the air mass to become warm. The warmed air expands, becomes lighter, and swirls up higher. This upward-swirling air carries dust and soot with it, leaving the lower air nice and fresh-smelling, and the sky clear and blue. A wonderful day for brisk outdoor fun—but not for flying. These columns of warm rising air make bumps and swirls in the air, and trouble for passengers with uneasy stomachs.

AIR MASS PICKS UP SOME WATER HERE

WHICH IT DROPS AS SNOW ON THE MOUNTAINS

2. Some of the air mass may sweep south over the Great Lakes and pick up some water vapor—not very much, because the air is cold. Still traveling south, the slightly moist air mass reaches the Appalachian Mountains and begins to climb, pushed ahead by the rest of the air mass behind it. As it climbs, the moist air becomes cooler. The higher up—the less squeeze—and the colder the air becomes. When it has climbed high enough and cooled enough, its water vapor freezes and drops down as snow flurries over the mountains. That same Polar Continental Air Mass, if it had swept over the Great Lakes in the summer, would have picked up a great amount of water vapor, enough to put on a good show. There would have been huge, billowy white clouds building higher and higher until a thunderstorm broke, with thunder and lightning to chase the hikers and mountain climbers back to town.

Canada is not the only weather-maker for us, nor is the Polar Continental the only air mass. There are eight others that make the weather for North America, and about a dozen more over the rest of the world. That's too much of a list to take up in detail, but let's look at three of the most important ones.

THESE ARE THE NINE WEATHER-MAKERS FOR NORTH AMERICA

TROPICAL GULF AIR MASS

This air mass is formed over the warm, sunlit waters of the Gulf of Mexico and the Caribbean Sea. The air here is calm and quiet for days on end, and the sun shines fiercely from directly overhead. Great quantities of water evaporate into the

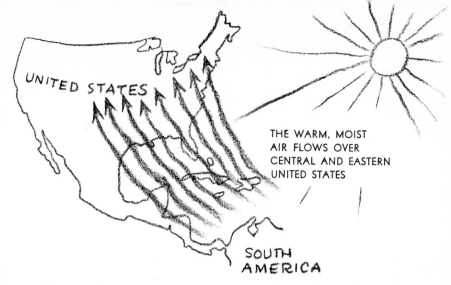

THE WARM, MOIST AIR FLOWS OVER CENTRAL AND EASTERN UNITED STATES

warm air. Then the warm, moist air mass finally moves, flowing north over the central and eastern United States. The kind of weather it brings depends upon several things, mainly the season of the year. When it arrives in winter, it finds cold land. The lower layers of the air mass, touching the cold land, are chilled into fog or low clouds that spread out flat and gray. The weather tends to stay put for quite a while without change. This is because the lower layers of air, having been chilled, have become heavier and stay down, so there is no up-and-down movement to stir the air.

IN WINTER THE AIR MASS IS CHILLED
INTO FOG OR LOW CLOUDS

In the summer, Tropical Gulf air brings warm, steamy weather that makes your clothes stick to you, and turns the sky hazy with water vapor. In the afternoons, when the sun has heated the land scorching hot, the lower layers of the warm moist air have become heated enough to expand and rise high. There they form the billowy clouds that give the afternoon thundershowers of summer.

POLAR PACIFIC AIR MASS

This air mass is a real traveler. Born in the Arctic regions, sometimes as far away as Siberia, it begins as a cold, dry air mass that sweeps across the North Pacific Ocean. On the way it picks up water vapor from the ocean, the amount depending on how long it takes to cross. Reaching this country along the northwest coast, it begins to

climb the Cascade Range of mountains nearby. As the air mass climbs, it meets thinner air and is able to expand and cool. With cooling comes condensation and rain that pours down the western side of the mountains. That side is well watered, with great forests and busy rivers.

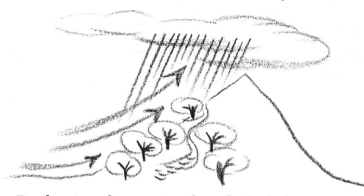

By the time the air mass has climbed the mountain peaks, most of its water vapor is gone. As it slides down the other side, it is squeezed and warmed, because now there is more air above it. It becomes a warm, dry wind, called a Chinook, that draws up water vapor from the ground as it blows eastward. Here the land is sparse and dry—cattle-grazing country. When the air mass reaches the Rocky Mountains, it begins a second climb. Again it cools as it rises, sprinkling the western sides of the mountains (but not showering because it didn't pick up much

CASCADES   ROCKIES

water). Again it slides down the other side, becoming compressed and warmed by its descent to lower altitudes. The warm air keeps going, drinking up moisture in summer and melting snows in spring. (It has been nicknamed "the snow-eater.") Sometimes it may have enough push to continue clear across the country and out to sea, or it may die out on the Central Plains. In either case, it is a huge weather-maker for a large part of this country.

GREAT PLAINS

PATH OF THE "SNOW-EATER"

TROPICAL CONTINENTAL AIR MASS

Greece, Turkey, and Spain are all warm countries, with very mild winters. Yet all of them are as far north of the equator as New York City, and have the same number of hours of daylight as New York, and the same slant of the sun's rays. Why is their weather so much milder?

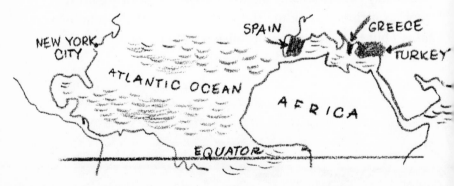

One reason for the warm weather in these European countries is the Tropical Continental Air Mass. This hot, dry air mass is formed in northern Africa, in the huge Sahara Desert, from which it sweeps north over the Mediterranean Sea into Europe. Bringing warmth and rain, it makes southern Europe a balmy, pleasant land of olive groves and fruit orchards, vineyards and seaside resorts.

There are many other air masses that make the world's weather, but these few examples are enough to show you what a vital part they play in people's lives. Farmland would become dry desert, and dry desert would turn into farmland, if the air masses that flow over each were exchanged.

WHAT MAKES AN AIR MASS TRAVEL?

Today is Bargain Day, Two for the Price of One. When you find out what sends an air mass on its travels, you will also know the answer to the question that began this chapter—why is it possible to predict the weather a long time in advance in tropical countries and near the Poles, but not in the temperate zones?

We'll have to find the answer one step at a time. Let's imagine that the earth is a perfectly round ball, with no mountains and no seas—just flat level land everywhere in the world. On such an earth you would find a belt of

COLD AIR   NORTH POLE

WARM AIR

COLD AIR   SOUTH POLE

warm air around the middle, where the sun's rays are the most direct. You would find a cap of cold air at the north pole and south pole, where the rays are most slanting. Between the belt and the two caps, in the temperate zones, the air would blend from warm to cold. All in all, a neat simple kind of world. Now come the complications.

Complication number one: the earth is not heated evenly all year round. Winter at the north pole, for example, is a time of no sunlight whatever, month after month. During this time the cap of cold air grows bigger, colder, and heavier, and begins to bulge and spread into the temperate zone. At the tropics, too, the sunlight is not the same all year. At certain seasons there are more hours of sunlight each day. At these times the belt of warm air grows wider and spreads farther.

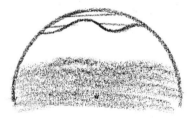

DURING OUR WINTER, THE CAP OF COLD AIR SPREADS DOWN

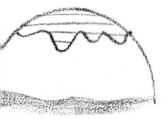

WHEN THERE ARE MORE HOURS OF SUN, THE BELT OF WARM AIR SPREADS

So then, on our neat imaginary earth, we could expect the cold caps to bulge into the temperate zones during the winter, and the warm belt to do the same in summer. The weather would change evenly and regularly from season to season, from cold to hot and back to cold again. But along comes complication number two, which makes the seasons change in bumps and surprises, with sudden cold spells in summer and warm spells in winter.

The earth is not a smooth even globe. It is full of ridges and hollows, mountains and valleys, land and water, sea breezes and monsoons, and winds set up by the spinning of the earth—all kinds of things that disturb the even spreading out of the cold caps in winter and the warm belt in summer. In one place a spreading cold cap is cut in two by the sharp ridge of a mountain range. In another a portion of the warm belt is bent to one side by a monsoon. In many parts of the temperate zones the bulging air is swung sideways by forces produced by the earth's spin. All these disturbances working together cause the air in the belt and the caps to be skimmed away and chopped off in blobs and whirls.

These blobs and whirls are air masses! When they break off, they go swirling along in a flow toward the east. Often, however, they do not break off, but bulge forward in a wave-like form that is pushed eastward and gradually smoothed down as it travels. We notice, too, that when a wave from the belt pushes forward, it causes part of the cap to be pushed inward. We can say this another way: when a tropical air mass pushes north, it generally causes the retreat of a polar air mass. A push by a polar mass will likewise cause the retreat of a tropical mass. And all this advancing and retreating across the temperate zones is what gives them their parade of weather—their wet spells and dry spells, their heat waves and cold waves, their constant surprises.

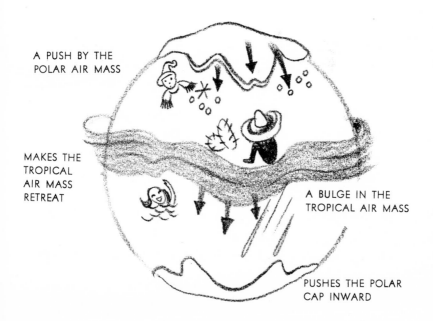

A PUSH BY THE POLAR AIR MASS

MAKES THE TROPICAL AIR MASS RETREAT

A BULGE IN THE TROPICAL AIR MASS

PUSHES THE POLAR CAP INWARD

The answers were a long time coming, but now we have them at last, although not nearly as completely as the weatherman has them. Let's get them down, together with the questions.

1. What makes air masses travel? They bulge outward from the belt and the caps, into the temperate zones. As they bulge out, they are bent and chopped and sent spinning by the winds and roughnesses of the turning earth.

A SOLID BANK OF WARM AIR IN THE TROPICS   MIXED WEATHER IN BETWEEN   A BANK OF COLD AIR AT THE POLES

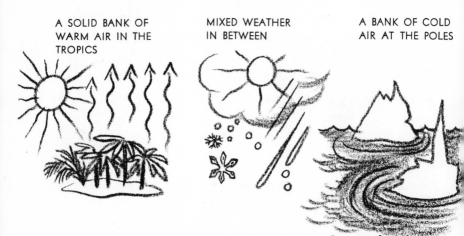

2. Why is it easier to predict the weather in the warm belt and the cold caps than in the temperate zones in between? Because the air in the tropics is fairly even, reliable stuff, a solid bank of warm air. And the air at the poles is a fairly reliable bank of cold air. But in between, in the temperate zones, it is anybody's guess, because things happen in fits and starts. The weather would change steadily and evenly if the earth were perfectly

smooth, with the surface entirely land or entirely water. But the mountain ranges, oceans, winds, and other differences on the earth's surface cause an uneven, unsteady change, with plenty of surprises to keep us from being bored.

This isn't the whole story, of course. There are many other "disturbers," each changing the weather in its own way. There are several smaller rivers of air between the equator and the poles, each changing the weather picture in its own small way. But now you know an important part of the story—how the air masses are made, and how they swirl along, bringing the weather of the world.

THE AIR MASSES HAVE A MEETING

YOU HAVE SEEN how air masses bring you packages of weather all the time. A Tropical Gulf Mass may settle itself in your part of the country, bringing day after day of broiling, steamy weather until, just when you think that you can't possibly take another day of it, the newspaper headlines announce: RELIEF IN SIGHT. BREAK DUE IN HEAT SPELL! That relief, most likely, is a Polar Continental Mass sweeping south, bringing cool dry weather once more. One after another, the air masses sweep over the country, delivering their packages of weather.

You have also seen that the actual weather you receive does not just depend on the kind of air mass that delivers it. It also depends on the kind of land that receives it. Hot land may receive a Tropical Gulf Mass in one way—thunder-showers in the afternoon, followed by clearing.

HOT LAND

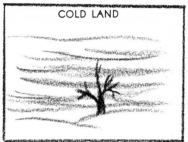

COLD LAND

Cold land may turn that same air mass into fog and low gray clouds that stretch for miles and miles. So the actual weather you get depends on the condition of the air mass *and* the condition of the land.

But your weather also depends on something else, and this is something that makes the liveliest weather of all— the meeting of air masses. Up to now we have been talking about air masses *already around you*. The cold spell brought by Polar Continental air takes place when the air mass has *already covered* the land. The same is true of Tropical Gulf's sticky weather, and the others as well. But air masses don't just suddenly appear around you. They have to travel to get there, and as they travel they have to push other air out of the way, or sometimes they get pushed out of the way themselves.

WARM   COLD

Wherever an air mass is advancing, some other air is retreating—a sort of Battle of the Airs. The battle front, the place where the two airs are pushing against each other, is even called a front. When a cold air mass advances against a warm mass, the front is called a cold front. An advancing warm mass pushing back a cold mass

WHEN A COLD AIR MASS ADVANCES
AGAINST A WARM AIR MASS THERE
IS A COLD FRONT

WHEN A WARM AIR MASS ADVANCES
AGAINST A COLD AIR MASS THERE
IS A WARM FRONT

is called a warm front. You can almost always tell when you are in the middle of a front, because the weather is usually quite lively and is then followed by a complete change. Let's see what happens.

HOW A COLD FRONT BEHAVES

Here is a picture of part of an advancing cold dry air mass. Only part can be shown because the whole thing is quite large, more than 700 miles from one side to the other, and over 10 miles high. If you could color it brown, it would look very much like a cookie, round (or sometimes oval) in shape, with a dome-shaped top, flat bottom, and rounded sides. Right now, we're interested in what is happening at the forward-moving part.

Let's assume that the advancing air mass is Polar Continental (cold and dry) and that it is pushing back a Tropical Gulf Mass (warm and moist). Along the front we can find all kinds of weather, one following the other. If you were actually there, you would be treated to each kind of weather in turn as the air masses moved over you.

1. The first piece of weather might be some light fog or general haziness, caused by chilling of warm moist air near the ground.

2. Next comes a pile of billowy thunderclouds, gray at the bottom, and a smashing shower that drenches the land. The clouds were formed of moisture from the warm, light air mass. This mass was lifted high by the heavy cold mass pushing under it, like snow lifted by a snowplow. Strong winds blow, caused by the violent circulation of warm and cold air. The powerful storm, that caught everybody by surprise, is over almost as suddenly as it began.

3. Everything begins to clear. Fewer and fewer clouds show in the sky, and soon the sun is out. The wind becomes gentle and the air is cool or cold.

A cold front shows itself by the weather changing from warmer to stormy to cooler.

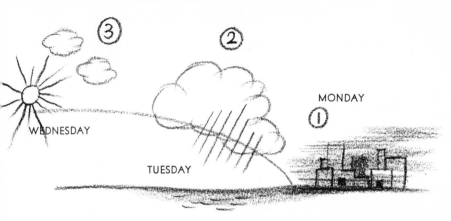

Now, if you knew the distance from 1 to 3 in the picture, and if you knew how fast the air mass was moving (they move about 500 to 750 miles in 24 hours), you could tell when each of these pieces of weather was coming. And if you knew where the air mass was going and how fast it was moving, you could call up the people living in its path and tell them, "Sudden storms coming, followed by clearing and cooler." In other words, you would have analyzed the conditions in the two air masses, and along the front, and predicted the coming weather. That's Weather Forecasting by Air Mass Analysis, and it's a large part of the weatherman's job.

Naturally, it isn't as simple as all that. To be accurate in his forecasting, the weatherman needs to know a great deal more about the two air masses than just the fact that one is cold and dry while the other is warm and moist, but now you have some idea of the kind of work involved in Air Mass Analysis.

Not every cold front puts on such an exciting show. If the cold mass is mildly cold, just slightly colder than the warm mass, the activity along the front will be less violent. The weather will change from mild to light rains to slightly cooler. And a cold front in wintertime will not behave exactly like a summer cold front. You may have snow or sleet instead of rain. But in spite of these differences, certain things happen in every cold front:

1. The clouds "climb a platform." That is, the first clouds are fairly low, or they may even be fog. The next, the thundercloud, will be somewhat higher, and if any clouds appear after that they will probably be as high or still higher.

2. The air becomes cooler and clearer after the cold air mass moves in.

HOW A WARM FRONT BEHAVES

A warm front looks and behaves quite differently. In a warm front, a large mass of warm air is pushing a cold mass. Since warm air is lighter than cold, the action is not like a snowplow that lifts the material in front of it. Instead it is a sort of squeezing ahead, as the picture shows. The cold air is squeezed backward by the advancing warm air mass.

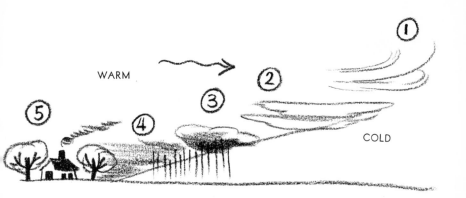

Let's look at the weather in a warm front. The advancing edge of the warm mass is high above the ground, so we can expect the first signs of the front to show themselves high up, and they do. We see feathery delicate bands or rows of clouds, very high in the sky. These (1) are called mare's tails, or cirrus clouds, and they are about eight miles up, where the air is so very cold that water vapor freezes. Those clouds are actually made of tiny ice crystals, formed out of vapor from the warm mass chilled by the cold mass. Several hours or half a day later, other clouds begin to appear. These (2) are thin, milky, and flat, like long white sheets. They are lower

than the mare's tail clouds, because they are formed along a lower part of the warm front. By now, it is definitely a cloudy day.

The slanting warm front keeps traveling forward, and the cloud layers are formed lower and lower (3). By now, they are dark gray, and a steady rain has begun to fall. It continues to rain, with lower and lower layers of dark clouds (4), until soon the clouds may be right around us—in other words, fog.

At last the warm front has passed (5) and the warm air mass itself has swept in and covered us. The air is warm and damp. In fact it may be doubly damp—first because of the rain evaporating from drenched fields and cities, and second because the warm air mass itself is moist.

Again, let's remember that this description of a warm front does not describe every single kind. The temperature of the land makes a difference; so does the kind of land, the season, and other things. But you can almost always expect two things with every warm front:

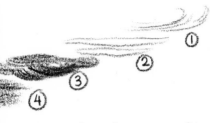

1. The clouds go "down the staircase." Each new cloud formation is lower than the one before, and is darker, more widespread, and gloomier.

2. After the warm front has passed, the weather is somewhat warmer and the air is clearer, but not brilliantly clear as in a cold air mass.

TWO AGAINST ONE

Sometimes a cold air mass overtakes another one, trapping a warm mass in between. The warm mass, being lighter, is heaved up on the shoulders of the two cold masses. Up high, with less squeeze on it, the air becomes cooler and chills its vapor. Down it comes as rain or snow, only to be followed by more cold weather.

Such a triple-mass arrangement is called an occluded front. It passes high above you, and these are the signs of its passage:

CLOUDS THAT OFTEN COME WITH A WARM FRONT

CIRRUS

CIRROSTRATUS

ALTOSTRATUS

NIMBOSTRATUS

STRATUS

CLOUDS THAT OFTEN COME
WITH A COLD FRONT

ALTOCUMULUS

CUMULONIMBUS

STRATUS

STRATOCUMULUS

1. The clouds in an occluded front go part way downstairs and then up. That is, they form lower and lower, and then higher and higher. The lowest clouds are usually some distance above the ground, and therefore you don't usually get clouds on the ground (fog) with this type of front.

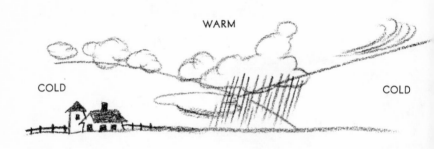

2. The weather goes from clear and cool, to stormy, to clear and cool.

No matter what type of front is passing, it always brings something a little special in the way of weather—clouds at various levels, rain or snow, perhaps fog. There's nothing dull about a front. And let's not forget winds, for they always come along with a front. The cold and warm air masses set up a speedy circulation, and you are treated to winds that suddenly flare up, change direction, and die down as one air mass leaves and the other comes in. Fronts are lively.

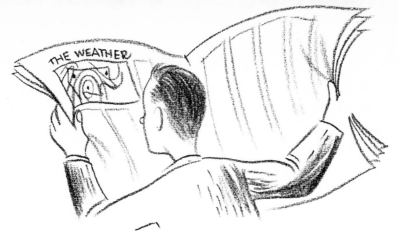

WEATHER MAPS AND HOW TO USE THEM

WHEN YOU WANT to know all the details about the weather conditions in some part of the country, you can ask somebody to write you an exact description in several thousand words. Or you can look at a weather map and get the whole story in a few numbers and symbols. What's more, the weather map will give you the weather information for the entire country. Even better, after you've learned how to read a weather map, you can do a fair job of forecasting some kinds of weather a day or two in advance.

Many newspapers publish a weather map every day. The map is supplied by the U.S. Weather Bureau, where it is made up by expert meteorologists, on the basis of information telegraphed in at the same time by over 400 weather observers throughout the country. The map in this morning's paper was made up during the night, but it can tell you tomorrow's probable weather, after you've had some practice.

A weather map looks rather bewildering when you see one for the first time, with all its looping lines and arrows and numbers. But if we take it one piece at a time, you'll find it quite simple.

ARROWS

We see something that looks like a queerly shaped arrow. One side of its tail is gone, and instead of a point it has a circle. This one little symbol gives us three pieces of information: direction of wind, speed of wind, and condition of sky. The wind direction is shown by the arrow itself, as if it were being blown by the wind. The arrow in the picture is pointing from west to east, indicating a wind from the west—a west wind. The number of lines on the tail of the arrow indicates the speed of the wind. The pictures at the side of this page show you what the lines mean in miles per hour. The filling-in in the circle tells you the sky condition— clear, cloudy, rain, etc.

CLEAR

PARTLY CLOUDY

CLOUDY

RAIN

SNOW

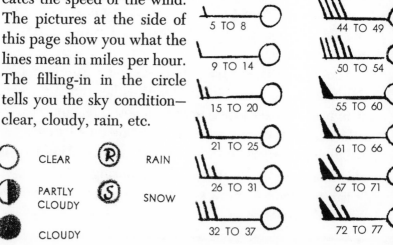

CALM

MILES PER HOUR

1 TO 4
5 TO 8
9 TO 14
15 TO 20
21 TO 25
26 TO 31
32 TO 37

38 TO 43
44 TO 49
50 TO 54
55 TO 60
61 TO 66
67 TO 71
72 TO 77

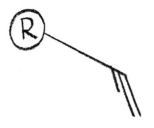

This arrow tells you that it is raining and that the wind is blowing from the southeast at a speed of between 26 and 31 miles per hour.

SHADING

Next, let's look at shading. This indicates that water in some form (rain, snow, sleet, or hail) has fallen in the shaded area some time during the previous six hours.

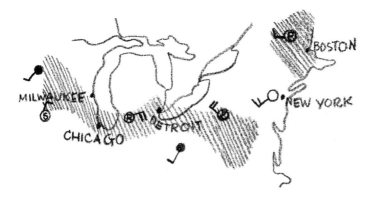

NUMBERS

Next, let us look at page 114. At the upper right of the arrow circle we see a number, 72. The temperature is 72 degrees Fahrenheit. Underneath it is the number .23. This means that 23 one-hundredths of an inch of rain has fallen in the last six hours. That is, if you had placed an empty straight-sided container (such as a tin can) out in the open six hours ago, it would now have water in it to a depth of 23 hundredths of an inch. No number in this space would mean that no rain had fallen in the past six hours.

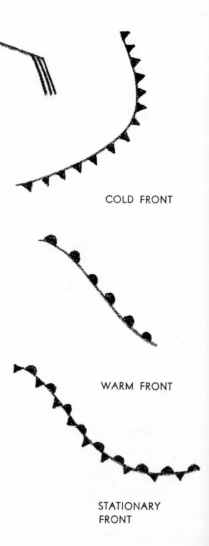

FRONTS

Now for the lines with teeth in them. The lines with pointed teeth mark a cold front—a place where a cold air mass is pushing back a warm mass. The points of the teeth show the direction in which the cold mass is advancing. This one is moving southeast. A warm front is shown by rounded teeth. This one is moving northeast. And here's a curious-looking one, with pointed teeth on one side and rounded teeth on the other. It shows a stationary front— the meeting place of a warm mass and a cold mass, neither one of which gives

COLD FRONT

WARM FRONT

STATIONARY FRONT

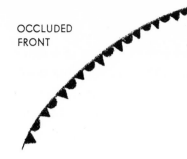

OCCLUDED
FRONT

way. And finally, a line with round and pointed teeth on the same side—an occluded front, where two cold air masses have lifted a warm mass "on their shoulders."

WHAT WILL THE WEATHER BE?

You're not finished with all the lines yet, but let's practice with the lines and symbols you've used this far.

On this map, your home town is Centerville, the day is Friday, the month is August, and you have a problem: "Shall I plan a trip to Lake Wharton on Lookout Mountain over the weekend, or shall I stay home and catch up on my reading?"

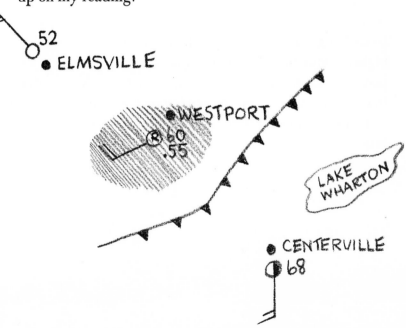

Well, let's see. If you judge by the weather in Center-ville things look pretty promising for an outdoor week-end. The air is a pleasant 68 degrees, and the wind is a gentle 8-to-12 miles per hour from the south, but that partly cloudy symbol is a bit disturbing. Will it clear up or become cloudier?

The answer is over toward the northwest, where a cold front is baring its teeth in our direction. That shaded area is rain. Notice that Westport has already had .55 inch in the last six hours. And it will probably be typical summer-cold-front rain—thunder-showers (though that's not on the map, but in what we know about air masses), followed by clearing, colder, and windy. Notice Elms-ville, which is all finished with its front weather, and now is having its cold mass weather—clear, 52 degrees, wind from the northwest at 25 to 31 miles per hour. And since Lake Wharton is up on Lookout Mountain, 2300 feet higher than Elmsville (again, that's not on the map, but just a matter of fact), we can expect it to be even colder than in Elmsville when the cold mass comes our way.

Thunder-showers *and* cold *and* windy—that's too much. Better stay home and read a book, this one, for instance.

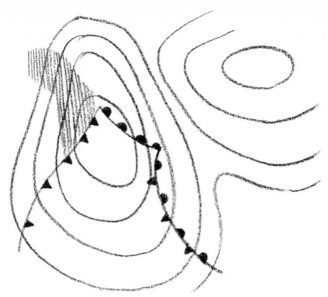

ISOBARS

Now, last but definitely not least, come the loopy, whirly lines called isobars, that run all over a weather map like giant fingerprints, or a drawing of an oyster shell. These lines help us to know what is going on *inside* the air masses. Let's look at the cold air mass that was responsible for canceling your weekend trip. Here it is:

It's a series of oval lines called isobars, each with a number attached, and the word HIGH in the center. The inside isobar has the number 1008, the next one 1005, the next 1002, and so on, each one 3 numbers lower than

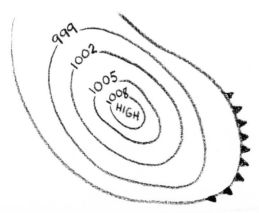

the previous one. These numbers refer to millibars, which are the weatherman's unit for air pressure. One thousand millibars are equal to about fifteen pounds.

Each number tells how strongly and heavily the air is pushing down, anywhere along its isobar line. Anywhere along the inner line, the strength of the air (let's call it air pressure from here on) is 1008, while anywhere along the next line it is 1005, and so on. As you can see, the highest pressure, the greatest push of air, is at the center, so that place is labeled HIGH, really meaning highest pressure or heaviest.

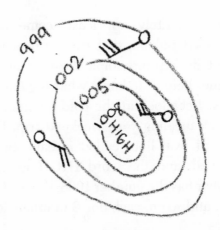

You know that heavy air is able to push less heavy air out of the way. As it pushes, it makes a wind. You can expect the winds in a cold air mass to blow from the heaviest air, the highest-numbered isobars, toward the general direction of the lowest-numbered isobars. And the arrows show they do.

Winds blow from higher pressure to lower pressure areas. Each isobar is three points different in pressure from the isobar next to it. If the isobars are far apart, the pressure change is gradual, and the wind is gentle. Where the isobars are close together, the pressure change is more sudden, so the winds are faster.

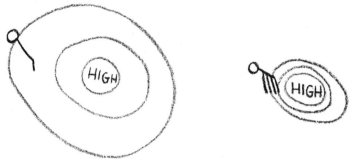

UNUSUAL WEATHER

Here's a little sample on which to try out these ideas. This collection of isobars is the picture of a very special piece of weather that happened along Florida. The numbers on each isobar tell the air pressure. The outside isobar shows 1005 millibars, the next is 1002, the next is 999, and so on, less and less, until we reach the place of lightest air or lowest pressure in the center, marked LOW. According to this isobar picture we can expect to

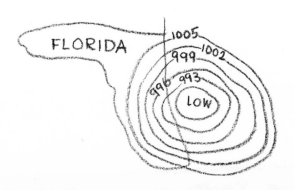

find air flowing from the outside isobars (heavy air) toward the center (lightest air). And at the center we should expect to see a column of warm rising air being pushed up by this inrushing cold heavy air.

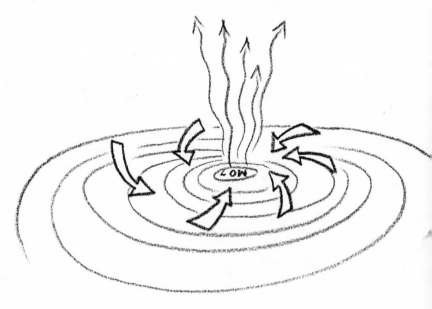

Well, let's look at that for a moment. The isobars are close together, so the wind is rapid. A column of warm rising air, being pushed up by cooler air rushing violently in from all sides—that sounds like either a tornado or a hurricane. Which is it? Notice the outline of Florida on the map; this piece of weather is much bigger than the whole state, so this couldn't be a tornado, which is violent but quite narrow. It can be a hurricane. And

that's what it is—the hurricane of Sept. 13, 1944, that began in the Caribbean Sea and swept north along the coast, smashing, wrecking, flooding, as it whirled northeast and out to sea; and on the map it looks so harmless, just a collection of isobars! Of course the Weather Bureau had been watching that low for days, and had sent out constant storm warnings that saved many lives.

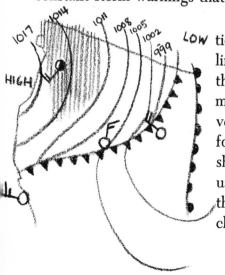

There's a lot of information we can read from isobar lines. The most important is the shape and size of air masses. This information is very important in weather forecasting, because the shape of an air mass helps us to locate its front, where there is always an abrupt change in weather. The size gives us one way to determine how long the weather will stay the same. A large mass will usually take longer to travel through an area than a small mass. The closeness of the lines tells us how violently the weather will change when the front of the air mass sweeps over us.

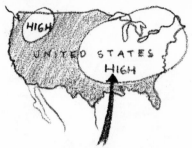

THIS MASS WILL TAKE A LONG TIME TO TRAVEL THROUGH AN AREA

So you see, a weather map can tell you a great deal about the weather, where it came from, where it is now, and where it's going. You can learn to read past, present, and future weather—for your part of the country and the rest of the country as well. Of course, you can't become a weather prophet just by looking at one map, but if you spend a few minutes each day studying the day's map in the newspaper, you will begin to see that the weather doesn't "just happen"—that you can see it coming and make your plans accordingly.

To get the most fun and use out of weather maps, keep a series of three or four on a bulletin board. Each day add the latest and remove the oldest. In this way you will have a continuously changing picture of the weather. And each day, when you put up the latest map, compare it with the previous two days and try to forecast tomorrow's weather.

As you look at your weather maps, you will soon notice that the weather often marches from west to east. Today's weather in a place five or six hundred miles west of you will probably be tomorrow's weather for you. This will help you with your weather forecasting.

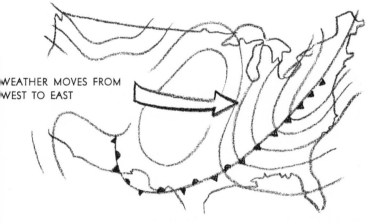

WEATHER MOVES FROM
WEST TO EAST

After you have made your prediction, read the Weather Bureau's forecast, which is usually printed right underneath the map. The chances are that you and the Weather Bureau will not usually be in complete agreement, but with practice you'll get better and better.

SCIENCE
HELPS THE WEATHERMAN

WHEN YOU LOOK at a weather map to see what kind of weather is on the way, perhaps you only think of how the weather affects you. In the summer, you may wonder if it will be nice enough for a picnic. Will it rain? Will it be warm enough to swim? Will it be too hot to run? In the winter you may be planning to ice skate or to ski. Will it snow? What should you wear?

Wouldn't it be nice to have the answers to these questions in advance? Certainly, it would make life more pleasant and this is one of the reasons why the Weather Bureau tries to give you the answers beforehand. But that isn't the only reason why millions of dollars are spent each year in preparing forecasts.

Suppose you were in the business of selling umbrellas or snow shovels. Suppose you were managing a trucking company or flying an airplane. Can you see how important a weather forecast might be?

But even more important is the fact that weather forecasts can save human lives! Let us look at some of the newer ways in which science helps the weatherman to warn us to protect ourselves far in advance of an approaching storm.

You would think it a simple matter to predict the path of a hurricane if you knew its location, the direction in which it was going, and how fast it was traveling. However, this is far more difficult than it seems.

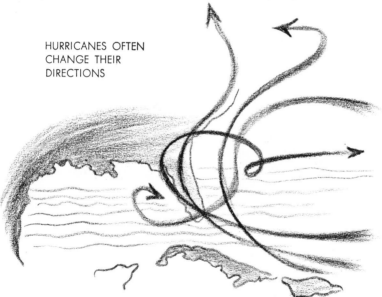

HURRICANES OFTEN
CHANGE THEIR
DIRECTIONS

For one thing, these violent storms begin far out at sea and, unless there are ships in the area, it is hard to know when a storm has started. Secondly, hurricanes are temperamental. They often change their speed and direction. This means they must be watched very closely.

While most of us would run from a hurricane if we could, there are some men who look for these tropical storms, ride right into them and follow them until they die down. They are the heroic hurricane hunters of the U.S. Navy and Air Force.

Imagine flying an airplane into winds of more than 150 miles an hour. The aircraft bobbles around like a cork on the sea, sometimes almost completely out of control as flying instruments go haywire in the storm. Often the crews of these weather planes must hold on for dear life as the air tears at the wings and bounces their craft around like a crazy kite. Yet, thousands of these hurricane flights have been made since weather reconnaissance first began in 1944. Surprisingly, only a few planes have been lost while a great deal has been learned about these terrifying storms.

Pilots in giant B-50 weather planes have learned how to fly into hurricanes with greater safety. New instruments have been developed to help them keep track of what goes on.

RADAR

One of the weatherman's instruments is radar, which is a kind of radio wave. It works something like this. Radio waves of a special type are beamed out from a transmit-

ter. When these waves strike something solid they bounce back. A rotating antenna picks up these reflected waves and they are then changed into pictures which are viewed on a screen like your TV.

During World War II, radar was used to track enemy planes and ships. Sometimes the weather interfered with these observations because raindrops and snowflakes reflect radar waves quite well. This difficulty was turned to an advantage when weathermen realized that radar could also be used to track the weather.

There are radar screens in many weather stations around the country. But radar works only for a distance of 150 to 200 miles. However, a radarscope in a weather plane flying close to a storm enables the flying radar operator to see how far the storm extends and which way it is moving.

Radar can also be used to study the winds in a thundercloud. The winds themselves will not bounce back radar waves, so a balloon is sent up carrying a box full of lightweight scraps of aluminum foil. When these are released, the radarscope can follow the aluminum pieces as they swirl about blown by the winds in the thundercloud. Thus the direction and force of these winds can be measured.

ALUMINUM SCRAPS

DROPSONDE

Another device used in the weather plane is the drop-sonde. Do you remember the radiosonde which is carried aloft by a balloon and sends back weather information by radio as it floats to the ground? The dropsonde is almost the same except that it is dropped by parachute from a weather plane. This has an advantage over the radiosonde because the pilot can release the dropsonde exactly where he pleases. Radio signals are then picked up by a receiver in the plane and the weather observer learns a great deal about the temperature, winds, moisture, and air pressure as the dropsonde descends.

PINPOINTING A HURRICANE

While tracking hurricanes with aircraft and radar has become easier and more accurate in recent years, one of the problems that still exists is that of locating a storm as soon as it starts.

New instruments are coming into use. Recently, Navy scientists discovered that hurricanes are so violent they actually shake the earth. Since this is so, very sensitive "earthquake" recorders have been set up in weather stations along the coasts to detect the beginnings of tropical storms.

Another storm detector is the hurricane buoy. Many of these buoys have been set out to float in areas off our southeastern coast. Instruments within the buoys measure air pressure, winds, the height of waves, and other signs of a brewing storm. This information is sent by built-in radio transmitters to nearby weather stations.

Since the southeastern tip of the United States is closest to the birthplace of most American hurricanes, the Weather Bureau in Miami Beach, Florida, has a special Hurricane Warning Center. When the first signs of a storm are radioed here from ships, planes, hurricane buoys, or other devices, the Bureau goes into action.

Weather squadrons at air bases in Florida, Bermuda, and Puerto Rico are alerted by radio. Assignments are made and giant B-50's are soon flying in search of the storm. Once the trouble is located, regular flights are made into the hurricane at six-hour intervals. The pilots work their way toward the calm "eye" of the storm, drop-

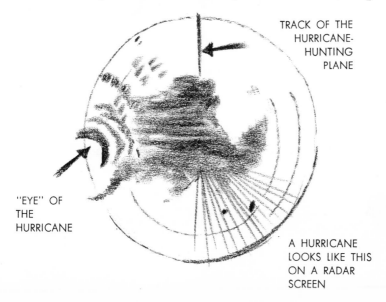

TRACK OF THE HURRICANE-HUNTING PLANE

"EYE" OF THE HURRICANE

A HURRICANE LOOKS LIKE THIS ON A RADAR SCREEN

sondes are released, and radar is beamed out. Soon the weather observer on board has a great deal of information about the location of the storm, its strength, its speed, and its movement to radio back to Miami. Within minutes this information is being teletyped to weather stations all along the coast.

Bulletins are broadcast by radio and TV to warn areas in danger. Storm warnings, red flags with square black centers, are hoisted along the seacoast. Weatherwise residents, warned in advance, can board up windows, shelter animals, ships, planes, automobiles, and themselves. Isn't it easy now to understand why fewer lives are lost in a hurricane nowadays than fifty years ago?

WEATHER SATELLITES

Have you ever looked down on the ground from a window high up in a very tall building? You can see people walk, watch the traffic below, even spot trouble before it happens. In some of our larger cities, police helicopters often fly over busy highways so that tie-ups can be spotted and reported by radio to officers on the ground. How wonderful it would be to be able to watch the weather in the same way. Imagine being up high enough to see much of the ocean at once, to see storm clouds gather and move along. Such has always been the weatherman's dream and now this dream is becoming a reality.

In October, 1957, the Russians successfully launched the first man-made satellite, a little moon that circled the earth at the almost unbelievable speed of 18,000 miles per hour. This was in the beginning of the space age and since that time dozens of satellites have been rocketed into space from all parts of the world. One of the most valuable in increasing our knowledge is our weather satellite, Tiros I, which was sent aloft in the spring of 1960.

The name Tiros comes from Television and Infra-Red Observation Satellite. Tiros I had no infra-red equipment aboard, but its twin television cameras picked up weather information never before seen. The satellite was active for about two and a half months and in that time almost 23,000 pictures were sent back to receivers on earth as Tiros I circled the globe every 100 minutes.

Some of these pictures revealed a peculiar square-shaped cloud which carried with it four tornadoes. Others showed typhoons in the Pacific and air movements never known before. Weather forecasters were delighted with the performance of Tiros I and, a few months later, Tiros II was sent into orbit 400 miles above the earth.

TYPHOON

One of the two TV cameras on Tiros II failed to work, but the second camera as well as other devices worked fine. Tiros II was equipped with infra-red equipment which can measure how much heat comes up from the earth, how much is reflected by clouds, and how much is absorbed. This kind of knowledge is precious to the weather scientist.

Weathermen are looking forward to a network of six or eight weather satellites in the near future which will scan the skies from above and report back to earth. These will have radar to measure the thickness of clouds, and other instruments to enable them to locate the beginnings of thunderstorms, hurricanes, and tornadoes.

No doubt, information from these weather "eyes" will be fed into computers, and weather maps will be constructed by electronic machines in minutes. Weather forecasting will be more scientific and more accurate than ever.

Perhaps, some day, we may know enough about the weather to make it behave as we want. Sunny days for play, rain for the farmer, snow in the country for sportsmen, calm winds for the sailor. Take your pick!

However, man-made weather is still in the future. Meanwhile, we had better stick to predicting tomorrow's weather with the maps and instruments we have today.

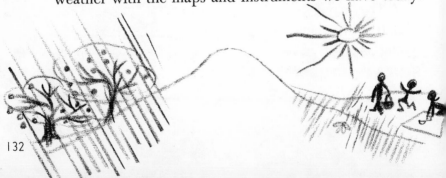

BUILDING YOUR OWN
WEATHER STATION

YOU CAN LEARN a lot from weather maps, especially if you keep a regular watch on them day after day. But weather maps, no matter how carefully prepared, have two limitations:

1. They are always slightly "behind the time." The map in this morning's paper was prepared last night.

2. They cover general conditions for large areas of the country, but they can't possibly tell you about what's going on right where you are, unless you happen to live near a weather station.

However, you can easily build a station of your own. Then your observations will be up to the minute, and they will give you information on the weather right where you are.

Of course, the instruments you build will not be extremely accurate, like the ones at the Weather Bureau that cost several hundred dollars apiece, but they are fun to build and can give you fairly good results.

The instruments for this weather station can be built with a hammer and a knife, and you can find most of the

materials in your home right now. To get the best use out of your weather station, make a record of your observations twice a day. A form for keeping such a record is shown on page 178. After several days or more of such observations, you will begin to see a "cause and effect" taking shape. You will see that today's weather is something that was brought on by that of yesterday and the day before, and so on. In the same way, yesterday's weather and today's are busy making tomorrow's weather. You can get some advance information from your homemade weather station.

MEASURING MOISTURE

HAIR HYGROMETER

A HAIR HYGROMETER (hi-grom′e-ter) measures the humidity, or moisture, of the air. This is a useful piece of information in forecasting the approach of a warm front, with its days of drizzle, and a cold front, with its quick showers followed by clear cool weather.

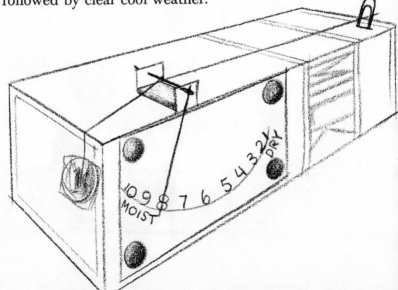

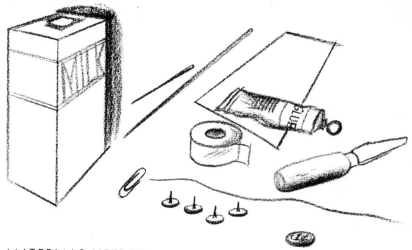

MATERIALS NEEDED

An empty milk carton washed out with cold water or a box of about that size, a sewing needle, a broom straw, scotch tape, a bit of nail polish or glue, a human hair at least nine inches long, four pins or thumbtacks, a sharp knife or razor blade, a blank card, a paper clip, and a penny.

HOW IT WORKS

Humid air causes the hair to stretch, while dry air makes it shrink. This change in length is very slight—you'd have a hard time measuring it with a ruler. But if this slight change is magnified, we can see it and make use of it. And that's what the needle and broom straw do—they magnify the change in size. When the hair shrinks a hundredth of an inch, the tip of the broom straw will move about 1¼ inches. That's a magnification of 125 to 1.

HOW TO BUILD IT

1. Wash the hair with soapy water or alcohol, and then rinse it in clear water and put it aside to dry.

2. With your knife, cut an H at one side of the carton.

3. Bend up the two tabs in the H, and punch a hole in each with your needle. Twist the needle around a bit, so that the holes permit the needle to turn freely.

4. Split off a piece of broom straw about three inches long, with one end just thick enough to push into the eye of the needle. Put a dab of nail polish or glue to fasten it there, and let it dry.

5. Cut a narrow slit at the far end of the carton, then push the paper clip half way in.

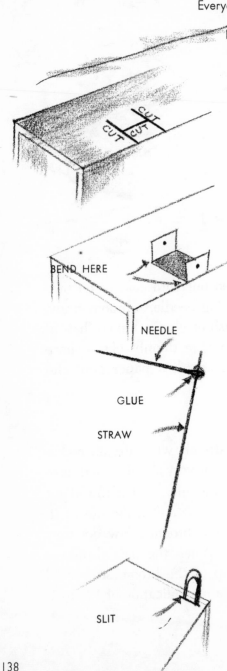

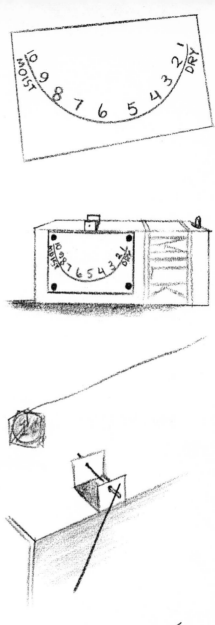

6. With compasses or a drinking glass as a guide, draw a half-circle on the card, and print the words DRY and MOIST as shown, and numbers 1 to 10 along the half-circle.

7. With four pins or thumbtacks, fasten the card to the carton.

8. With scotch tape, fasten one end of the hair to the penny. Try not to touch the rest of the hair, because the grease of your skin prevents the hair from absorbing moisture.

9. Place the needle and straw into the holes in the H tab.

10. Wind the hair around the needle, one turn from underneath and around. Slip the free end of the hair into the paper clip, and fasten it with a dab of glue or

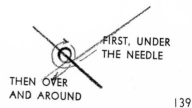

FIRST, UNDER
THE NEEDLE

THEN OVER
AND AROUND

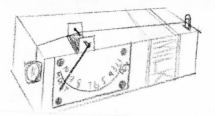

nail polish. The penny should hang about an inch over the end of the carton.

Now you're all ready, except for adjusting your hygrometer. The broom straw needs to be set to show the right humidity. There are two ways of doing this:

1. Set the hygrometer on a level surface in your bathroom. Turn on the shower and let it run until the mirror and windows cloud up. Now the air is full of water vapor, or 100 per cent humid. You will see the broom straw turn slowly as the hair stretches. It will finally come to a stop when the hair has stretched as far as it will in completely damp air. Now turn the broom straw so that it points to the number 10. Then carefully carry it out of the bathroom and set it gently in a shaded, protected place where you plan to keep it.

2. Another way of setting your hygrometer is to place it in a large metal container, such as a bucket, together with a damp washcloth next to it, and cover the bucket with a damp towel. After fifteen minutes, take off the towel and immediately set the pointer to number 10.

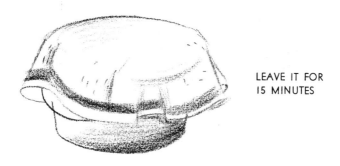

LEAVE IT FOR
15 MINUTES

HOW TO USE THE HYGROMETER

Your hygrometer shows the humidity of the air immediately around it. In seasons when the windows are open, the air in your house will be about as moist as the outdoor air in a shaded place, so you can keep your hygrometer indoors and yet be able to find out the humidity of the outside air. But when the windows are closed, you'll have

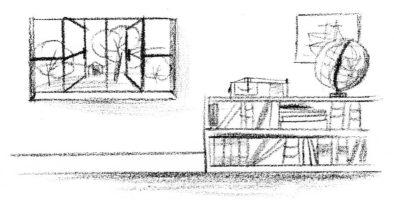

to keep your hygrometer outdoors, in a protected place out of the sunlight. Before taking a reading, tap the carton *gently* two or three times.

In order to use your hygrometer as a weather forecasting instrument, you should take readings at the same time every day. The same is true of the other instruments in your weather station.

In general, you will find that the humidity of the air increases before a rain and decreases afterward. When a front is approaching, the humidity will change as follows:

	Before front	*During front*	*After front*
Warm front	Increasing	Very moist	Slight decrease
Cold front	Steady	Very moist	Rapid decrease

WET-AND-DRY-BULB HYGROMETER

This is another type of hygrometer, with two advantages and one disadvantage over the hair hygrometer. It does not require setting of a pointer because there is no pointer, and it is quite accurate. However, it costs more because you have to buy two thermometers.

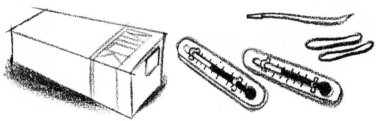

MATERIALS NEEDED

A clean milk carton, two rubber bands, and two thermometers. The cheap five-and-ten-cent-store thermometers will do, but get two that read as nearly alike as possible. You will also need a piece of wide, white cotton shoelace, about four inches long.

HOW TO BUILD IT

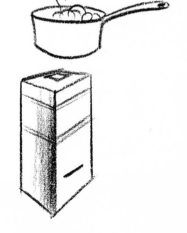

1. Boil the piece of shoelace for a few minutes, to wash out any chemicals that may be in it.
2. Cut a little slot in one side of the carton, about two inches from the bottom.

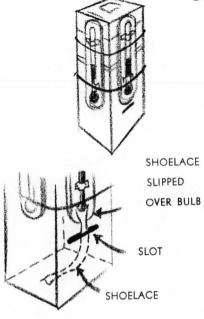

SHOELACE
SLIPPED
OVER BULB

SLOT

SHOELACE

3. Hold one thermometer on each side of the carton, and snap the two rubber bands around to hold them in place.

4. Then slip one end of the shoelace through the slot, into the carton, until it lies on the bottom. Push the other end around the bulb of one of the thermometers.

5. Then pour water into the carton through the top, almost as high as the slot. If you find that the instrument is tippy and tends to fall, it is because your particular thermometers are extra heavy. In that case stand it next to a wall, and push two pins through the upper corners of the carton into the wall.

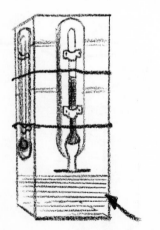

WATER

HOW IT WORKS

When you step out of a warm bath, you feel cool, even though the room may be quite warm. This is because water is evaporating from your skin. When water evaporates from something, it cools the thing from which it is evaporating. The faster the evaporation, the cooler you feel. When you go from the warm bathroom into your warm bedroom, you feel cooler still. This is because the bedroom air has less moisture in it, and can take up the moisture from your skin very quickly. We can put it this way: Dry air permits quick evaporation and produces lots of cooling. Moist air permits slow evaporation and produces less cooling. The dryer the air, the more cooling takes place.

WARM   COOLER   COOLEST

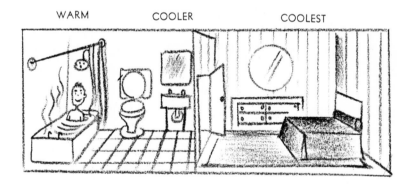

Your two thermometers can tell you how moist the air is—the humidity. The plain thermometer tells you the actual temperature of the air. The other thermometer, moistened by the wet shoelace, will read cooler, because it is being cooled by evaporation of water from the shoe-lace. The dryer the air, the more rapid the evaporation, and therefore the more cooling takes place. If the air were completely filled with water vapor, no water could evaporate from the shoelace. Then there would be no cooling of the thermometer, and both thermometers would read the same.

Your wet-and-dry-bulb hygrometer, when used with the table on page 147, will tell you the relative humidity of the air. This means the amount of water vapor in the air compared with the total amount that the air can possibly hold at that temperature. If the air contains half as much water as it can hold, the humidity is one half, or 50 per cent. One quarter as much, 25 per cent, and so on. When you take a shower, the relative humidity of the air in the bathroom is 100 per cent. The air can't hold any more water vapor than it already has in it. There is no room for the extra water vapor that keeps steaming out of the shower, so some of it condenses on the windows, mirrors, and walls of the bathroom, making everything damp and drippy.

Table of Relative Humidity

Difference between wet-bulb and dry-bulb readings	Temperature of air, dry-bulb thermometer, Fahrenheit							
	30°	40°	50°	60°	70°	80°	90°	100°
1	90	92	93	94	95	96	96	97
2	79	84	87	89	90	92	92	93
3	68	76	80	84	86	87	88	90
4	58	68	74	78	81	83	85	86
6	38	52	61	68	72	75	78	80
8	18	37	49	58	64	68	71	74
10		22	37	48	55	61	65	68
12		8	26	39	48	54	59	62
14			16	30	40	47	53	57
16			5	21	33	41	47	51
18				13	26	35	41	47
20				5	19	29	36	42
22					12	23	32	37
24					6	18	26	33

To use your wet-and-dry-bulb hygrometer, first note down the temperature of the dry thermometer. Then fan the wet-bulb thermometer for about fifteen seconds and note down its temperature. Subtract this number from the dry-bulb number. Now find this new number in the left-hand column of the table. Hold your finger there. Now, clear across the top of the table you will see degree numbers, such as 30°, 40°, etc. Find the number that is nearest to the dry-bulb number. Then go down that column until you come to the number that is on the same line as your finger. That number is the relative humidity in per cent. Let's try it.

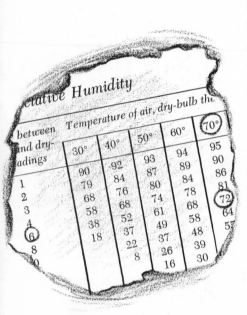

Relative Humidity

between and dry-bulb readings	Temperature of air, dry-bulb the				
	30°	40°	50°	60°	70°
1	90	92	93	94	95
2	79	84	87	89	90
3	68	76	80	84	86
4	58	68	74	78	81
6	38	52	61	68	72
8	18	37	49	58	64
		22	37	48	55
		8	26	39	
			16	30	

Suppose the dry-bulb number reads 71° and the wet-bulb 65°. Subtracting one from the other gives you the number 6. Put your finger on the 6 in the left-hand column. Now look at the degree numbers across the top until you come to the number that is nearest to your dry-bulb number—71°. The nearest number is 70°. Go down that column until you come to the number on the same line as your finger. That number is 72. The relative humidity of the air is 72 per cent.

That, by the way, is a nice figure for normal air. But in a heated house in the winter, the humidity sometimes drops to 30 per cent or even lower—much too dry for good breathing, because the thirsty air takes away lots of water from the lining of your nose and throat, leaving you with a dry, parched feeling.

In weather forecasting, you use the wet-and-dry-bulb hygrometer in the same way as the hair hygrometer, as explained on page 142. If you build both, you can use the wet-and-dry one as a guide for placing the proper humidity numbers on the dial of the hair hygrometer, instead of just having the numbers 1 to 10. To get the most accurate results, keep your hygrometer out in the open, but in a shaded place.

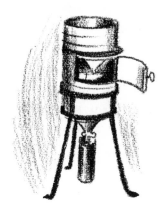

THE WEATHERMAN
USES THIS KIND
OF RAIN GAUGE

RAIN GAUGE

This instrument measures the amount of rainfall. Actually, any open container with straight sides can be used for measuring rainfall. All you need to do is stick a ruler into the water, zero end down, and see how far up the ruler becomes wet. If the ruler is wet up to the two-inch mark, then two inches of rain have fallen. The trouble with this method is that an ordinary rainfall is much less than an inch, and a light shower may be only a fiftieth of an inch.

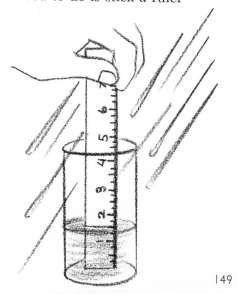

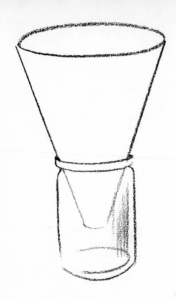

You would have a hard time measuring such slight amounts along an ordinary ruler. We need some way of magnifying the reading on the ruler, and we have such a way. We use a wide funnel pouring into a narrow jar. You will understand it better after you have built it.

MATERIALS NEEDED

A pointed paper cup, a ruler, a milk carton, a small straight-sided jar or medicine vial, a larger jar about the same size across as the paper cup, scotch tape, scissors, and a sheet of white paper.

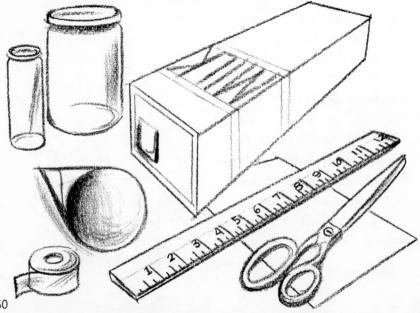

HOW TO BUILD IT

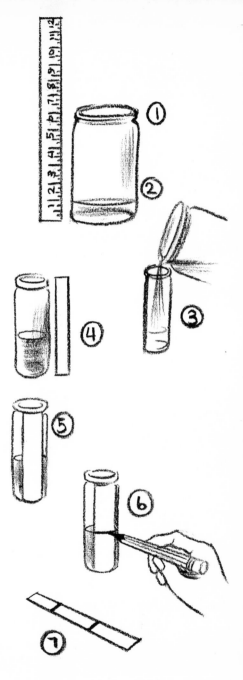

1. Place the ruler, zero end down, alongside the large jar.

2. Pour water into the jar until it reaches a height of one inch.

3. Then pour this water into the little jar.

4. Now cut a strip of paper about half an inch wide and as high as your little jar.

5. Place this strip against the outside of the little jar, with the bottom of the strip exactly alongside the bottom of the water in the jar.

6. Make a pencil mark on the paper, at the top of the water.

7. Now put the paper down on the table, and make another mark, the same distance from mark number one as that one is from the bottom of the strip.

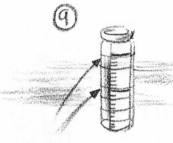

SCOTCH TAPE

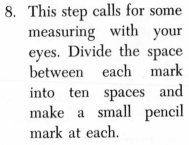

8. This step calls for some measuring with your eyes. Divide the space between each mark into ten spaces and make a small pencil mark at each.

9. Place your paper strip against the jar, with the marked side next to the glass, and fasten it by winding several strips of scotch tape around the jar.

10. Cut the tip off the paper cup, and the top off the milk carton. Also cut a large opening in one side of the carton, as in the picture.

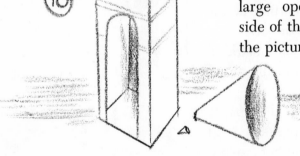

Now you're ready to assemble your rain gauge. Empty the little jar and put it inside the carton, with the paper strip to the back so that you can see the markings through the glass. Put the paper cup on top, and you're all set. To use your rain gauge, it's obvious that you'll have to place it out in the rain. It's best to put it inside a large can or bucket, because the whole gauge is rather light and can be blown over by a moderate wind.

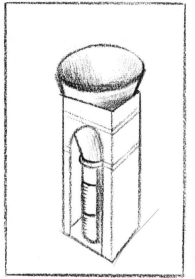
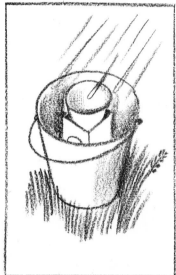

Once a day, measure the rainfall (if there has been any) by seeing what line the water level is up to, and then pour out the water. Each line marks a tenth of an inch of rainfall.

RAINFALL

You may be interested in a few statistics about rainfall. The state with the most rainfall is Louisiana, where about 55 inches fall during the year. That is if you had a straight-sided bucket 55 inches high, it would take a year for it to fill up with rain (assuming that no water evaporated, of course.) The least amount of rain falls in Nevada, about 9 inches a year. The average for the whole country is about 29 inches. Mt. Waialeale on Hawaii is the wettest place known with 471 inches yearly. Another place with a lot of rain is Cherrapunji, India—426 inches per year. That's wet indeed, especially when you consider that most of that rain falls during a few months in the rainy season. Once at Cherrapunji it rained 150 inches in five days! Those summer monsoons are great water-carriers.

WATCHING THE WIND

ANEMOMETER

YOU CAN ALWAYS recognize a weather station by its anemometer (an-e-mom′e-ter), (wind speed indicator) spinning cheerily. It consists of three cups (some types have four) mounted on arms that are free to spin. When the wind blows, it skims by the outside of each cup but is caught by the hollow inside, causing the whole thing to turn. The faster the wind, the faster the turning. The anemometer is electrically connected to a dial inside the weather station, showing the speed of the wind in miles per hour.

The anemometer for you to make is not nearly as elegant, but on the other hand you can build it in less than an hour, and the materials will probably cost nothing. It will be a very attractive part of your weather station.

MATERIALS NEEDED

Wire coat-hanger, milk carton, medicine dropper, four pointed paper cups, paper clips or stapling machine.

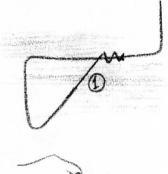

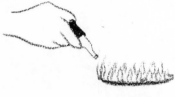

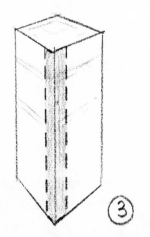

CUT OUT EACH CORNER
LIKE THIS

HOW TO BUILD IT

1. Untwist the coat-hanger. Break off the crooked ends. Then bend it into the shape shown in the picture.

2. Holding the medicine dropper by its rubber bulb, melt the glass tip over a gas flame or electric range. Turn the dropper as you heat it, so that it is heated evenly all around the tip. When you are through, the tip should be solidly closed. Then place it on a dish and allow it to cool for at least five minutes. Glass stays hot for quite a while, and can give you a scorching reception.

3. While the dropper is cooling, you can start cutting the arms of the anemometer. These are made by cutting a

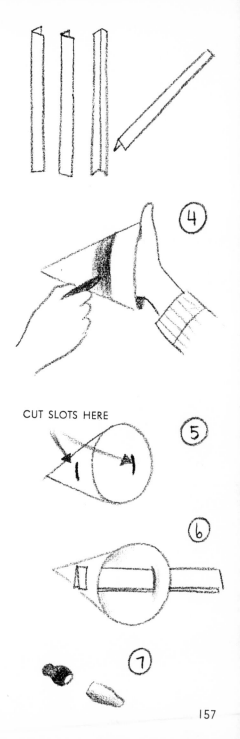

straight line, top to bottom, about three-fourths of an inch from the corner of the carton, and another line the same distance away on the other side of the corner. Cut four strips like this, one from each of the four corners.

4. With crayon make a large colored circle on the underside of one cup. This will make it easier to count the number of turns that the anemometer makes in a minute. (Did you ever hear about the man who used to count sheep by counting the number of legs and dividing by four?)

5. Cut two slots, three-fourths of an inch wide, in each of the paper cups.

CUT SLOTS HERE

157

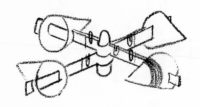

DROPPER

ONE SET OF ARMS
LOOKS THIS WAY
FROM THE TOP

NUMBER OF TURNS

IN 30 SECONDS

÷ BY 5

= WIND SPEED IN MILES PER HOUR

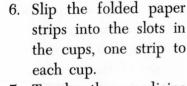

6. Slip the folded paper strips into the slots in the cups, one strip to each cup.

7. Touch the medicine dropper gently, to see if it is still hot. If it is cool, take the rubber bulb off.

8. With paper clips or staples (staples are better) fasten the arms and cups to the medicine dropper, as shown.

9. Slip the medicine dropper over the upright wire on the hanger, and that's that. The wind will take care of the rest. Your anemometer will whirl rapidly when the wind is strong, slowly in a light wind. But how do you determine the wind speed?

10. Here is a rough rule for finding the wind speed: count the number of turns in thirty seconds,

divide by five, and that will give you the wind speed in miles per hour If you want to get a more accurate system by actually testing your anemometer, here's how to do this.

11. On a calm day ask someone to take you for a ride in his car, on a quiet road. Sit next to the front right door, with the window open. (Make sure the door catch is locked.) Hold the anemometer out of the window and have the driver go a steady five miles per hour. As the car goes, count the number of turns in thirty seconds. Mark it down: 5 miles per hour— 27 turns (whatever it actually turns out to be). Then do the same at 10 miles per hour, and again at 15 and 20, each time writing down the numbers you get. From these figures you can make a graph that would look something like the following, but not exactly because each anemometer is a bit different.

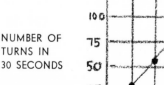

NUMBER OF TURNS IN 30 SECONDS

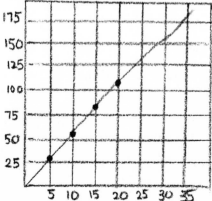

WIND SPEED IN MILES PER HOUR

Now you are ready to mount the anemometer outside or on the roof. Take everything outside—coat-hanger, medicine dropper, and arm-and-cup combination—plus a hammer and some U tacks. Nails will do if you have no U tacks. Fasten the bent coat-hanger to a pole, rod, or fence post out in the open, where the wind can blow against it.

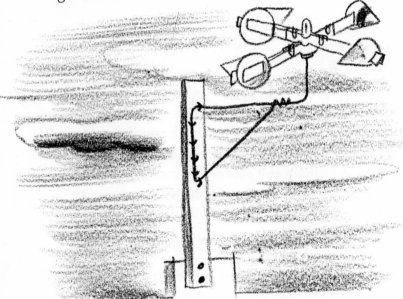

BEAUFORT SCALE

There is another way of determining the wind speed, but the results will not be very exact. This method was devised way back in the days of sailing ships, by an English admiral named Beaufort, and is called the Beaufort Scale.

The Beaufort Scale for Estimating Wind Speed

Beaufort number	Wind speed in miles per hr.	Description of wind in weather forecasts	Noticeable effect of wind on land
0	Less than 1	Calm	Smoke rises vertically.
1	1–3	Light	Direction shown by smoke drift, but not by vanes.
2	4–7		Wind felt on face; leaves rustle; wind vanes moved.
3	8–12		Leaves and twigs in motion. Wind extends a light flag.
4	13–18	Moderate	Raises dust and loose pages and moves small branches.
5	19–24	Fresh	Small trees in leaf begin to sway.
6	25–31	Strong	Large branches begin to move. Outdoor telephone wires whistle.
7	32–38		Whole trees in motion.
8	39–46	Gale	Twigs break off. Progress generally impeded.
9	47–54		Slight structural damage occurs. Hanging signs and television antennas blown down.
10	55–63	Strong gale	Trees uprooted. Considerable structural damage.
11	64–75		Damage is widespread. Experienced round the edge of hurricanes and tornadoes.
12	above 75		Countryside is devastated. Winds of this force are encountered only near the center of hurricanes, typhoons, etc.

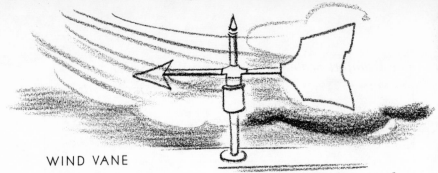

WIND VANE

This familiar instrument is commonly called a weather vane, but it really tells wind direction. It is true, however, that the direction of the wind will often tell you something about the coming weather.

MATERIALS NEEDED

Medicine dropper, milk carton, coat-hanger, paper clips or staples (staples are better).

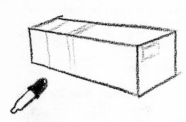 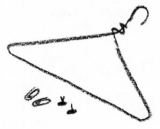

HOW TO BUILD IT

If you have built the anemometer, you will find this one quite simple, because the parts are made the same way.

TIP CLOSED

1. Make a coat-hanger bracket just like the one made for the anemometer.
2. Prepare the medicine dropper in the same way.

162

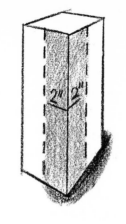

3. Cut a double strip of paper from the corner of the carton, similar to the strips used for the arms of the anemometer, but this one should be two inches from the corner each way. In other words, this strip will be four inches wide and as long as the milk carton.

4. Cut this double strip into the shape of an arrow, as shown.

5. Push the tube of the medicine dropper between the two parts of the arrow, closer to the point of the arrow than to the tail. Fasten it in place with paper clips or staples.

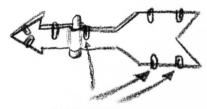

PAPER CLIPS

6. With nails or U tacks, fasten the coat-hanger bracket to the post, above the anemometer and to one side.

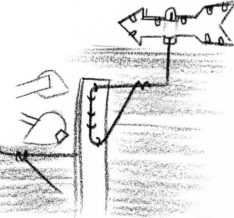

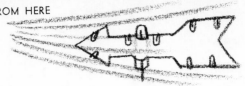

Your wind vane is simple, but will work quite well. It will point to the direction *from* which the wind is blowing, because the tail side of the arrow is larger than the point side, and catches more wind.

As you keep daily records of wind direction, you will find that certain directions often bring certain kinds of weather. For a starter, here is a short list of winds, together with the weather they usually bring:

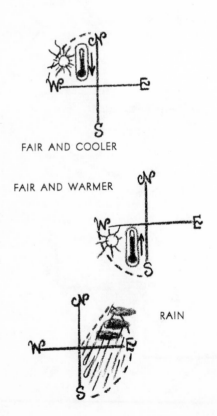

FAIR AND COOLER

FAIR AND WARMER

RAIN

FOR THE EASTERN AND CENTRAL UNITED STATES

Winds coming from the north, northwest, or west, usually bring fair and cooler weather because they come from cooler land farther north or from dry land farther west.

Winds from the west, southwest, or south usually bring fair and warmer weather because they come from warmer land.

Winds from the south, southeast, east, and northeast bring rain. These winds usually blow in from the ocean.

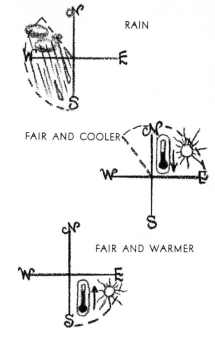

FOR THE WEST COAST OF THE UNITED STATES

Winds from the south, south-west, west, and northwest, blowing from the ocean, usually bring rain.

Winds from the north-west, north, northeast, and east usually bring fair and cooler weather from cooler land.

Winds from the east, southeast, and south usually bring fair and warmer weather from warmer land.

You may have noticed that there is some overlapping of winds. For example, northwest winds are mentioned twice, bringing rain or fair and cooler weather. Let's keep in mind that this is just a *very* rough guide to give you a general idea. Your own observations will help you become more expert in forecasting weather from wind directions.

CLOUD DIRECTION INDICATOR

Your wind direction indicator, or weather vane, tells the direction of the wind *near the ground*. But this wind is only the bottom part of the whole wind; there is more of it above you, and it is not necessarily moving in the same direction as the bottom part. Hills, trees, houses, and other obstructions sometimes cause the air to swirl and

change direction, like the water flowing around a boulder in a brook. To find the true direction of the wind, the weatherman sends up a gas-inflated balloon and watches it through a special telescope. The balloon, as it rises, is carried along by the wind. By watching the way the balloon goes, the weatherman can tell which way the wind goes.

You probably don't own any such balloons or telescopes, but there are usually some ready-made balloons in the sky—the clouds. They move with the moving air, so if you watch them as they drift by, you can tell the true wind direction.

However, it's a little difficult to crane your neck and try to guess direction, so here's a little cloud direction indicator, a nephoscope (nef'o-scope), to make the job easier and more accurate.

MATERIALS NEEDED

A round mirror, a sheet of white cardboard larger than the mirror, and a small piece of gummed paper.

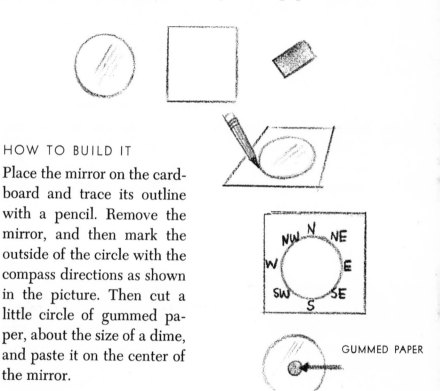

GUMMED PAPER

HOW TO BUILD IT

Place the mirror on the cardboard and trace its outline with a pencil. Remove the mirror, and then mark the outside of the circle with the compass directions as shown in the picture. Then cut a little circle of gummed paper, about the size of a dime, and paste it on the center of the mirror.

HOW TO USE IT

Set the card on a level place outdoors, with the N mark to the north. (If you aren't sure of compass directions in your locality, you will find instructions in the next paragraph). Place the mirror on it, exactly fitting the circle you drew. Look for clouds in the mirror. When one ap-

pears, choose a little tuft or curl that passes over the gummed paper, and follow it until it reaches the edge of the mirror. At the edge you will see the wind direction indicated on the card. This is the direction *toward* which the wind is blowing. If it is blowing toward the west, it is coming from the east—an east wind.

HOW TO FIND NORTH

In order to know the wind direction, you first need to know direction—north, east, south, and west—where you are. A compass will give you the approximate direction of north, but you can get it more exactly in the following way.

MATERIALS NEEDED

This job will take about 30 minutes, and should be started at about 11:30 A.M. standard time, or 12:30 daylight-saving time on a sunny day.

Take two straight sticks, three or four feet long, and a crayon or pencil to mark the sticks. Set one stick upright in the ground. Look for its shadow on the ground, and place the other stick right in the shadow, with one end right against the upright stick. Make a mark on the lying-down stick, at the place where the shadow ends. In three or four minutes the shadow will have moved. Move the stick until it is in the shadow again, but keep its end against the upright stick. Again mark the end of the shadow. You will find that the second mark is closer to the upright stick. Keep moving the stick as the shadow moves, and keep marking the end of the shadow on the stick. Each new mark will be closer and closer to the upright stick, until you suddenly come to a point where the marks stop coming nearer and start to move away. Just before that point is true north. The stick on the ground is pointing north.

SHADOW

(1)

(2) SHORTEST SHADOW

THIS IS NORTH

(3) SHADOW GETS LONGER

ANEROID
BAROMETER

THE WEATHERMAN'S
BAROMETER LOOKS
LIKE THIS

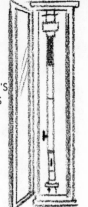

EXAMINING THE AIR

BAROMETER

THE WEATHERMAN finds this the most useful of all his instruments. A barometer (ba-rom'e-ter) tells you the pressure of the air—how heavily it presses. Cold air has more pressure than warm air, so an increase in pressure usually indicates the approach of weather that is cooler —and drier. It is drier because cold air holds less water vapor than warm air.

A very accurate barometer is expensive, thirty dollars or more. But you can get fairly good results with a home-made one. Here are directions for building a barometer out of scrap materials.

MATERIALS NEEDED

A milk carton, an empty tin can small enough to fit into the carton, a small sheet of plastic (the kind used for

making shower curtains, tablecloths, etc.) or a piece of balloon, a paper clip, a needle, thread, nail polish or cement, a broom straw, a white card, scotch tape, paper match, two thumbtacks, two pennies.

HOW TO BUILD IT

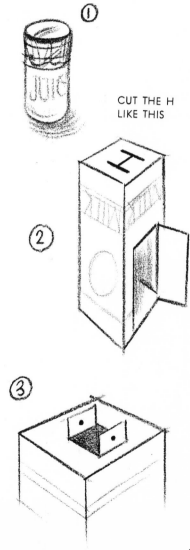

CUT THE H
LIKE THIS

1. Cut a circle of plastic sheet or rubber, about two inches larger than the bottom of the tin can. Stretch the sheet over the open end of the can, neatly and without wrinkles, and fasten its edges to the side of the can with several layers of scotch tape or a few rubber bands.

2. Cut a door in the side of the carton and an H at the bottom.

3. Turn up the flaps of the H. With your needle, bore a hole in the center of each flap. The holes should be large enough to permit the needle to turn freely.

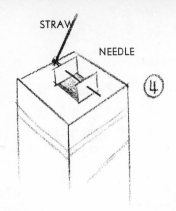

STRAW

NEEDLE

4. Cut a thin piece of broom straw about three inches long, and push one end through the eye of the needle. Fasten it with a dab of nail polish or cement.

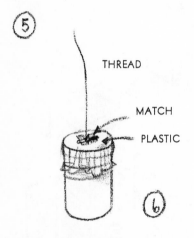

THREAD

MATCH

PLASTIC

5. Cut a piece of thread about 10 inches long. Tie one end around a small piece of paper match. Then attach the piece of match to the center of the plastic sheet, using scotch tape, cement or nail polish.

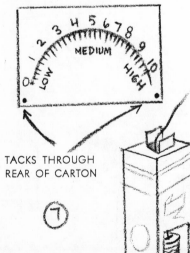

0 1 2 3 4 5 6 7 8 9 10
LOW MEDIUM HIGH

TACKS THROUGH REAR OF CARTON

DOOR

6. Draw a half-circle on the card, with the words HIGH, MEDIUM, and LOW, and the numbers 1 to 10, as shown. Attach the card to the carton with thumbtacks.

7. Put the tin can inside the carton and pass the thread through the hole made by the flaps.

8. Push the needle and straw through the holes

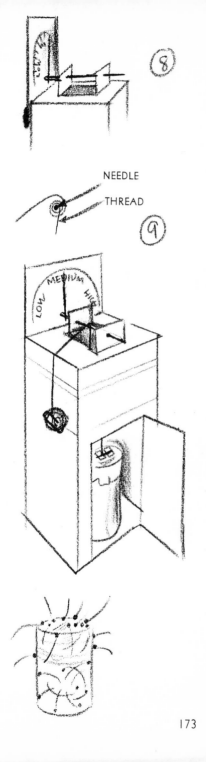

in the flaps, until the straw is near but not quite touching the card.

9. Wind the thread around the needle—over from the right side, twice around and over the edge of the carton. Tie the loose end to a paper clip and slip two pennies into the clip. Their weight will keep the thread taut. Set the broom straw straight up, pointing to the word MEDIUM.

HOW YOUR BAROMETER WORKS

The molecules of air in the can bounce around in all directions. Those near the top bounce against the plastic sheet. This would make the sheet bulge upward, but other molecules of air above the sheet are pushing it down, so the sheet stays level. But when the outside

WHEN THE OUTSIDE AIR
IS HEAVY, THE SHEET
IS PUSHED DOWN

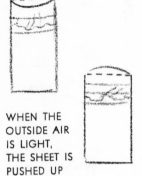

WHEN THE
OUTSIDE AIR
IS LIGHT,
THE SHEET IS
PUSHED UP

air becomes heavier and presses harder, the sheet will be pushed down a bit. When the outside air becomes weak, the sheet will be pushed up slightly by the air inside. These movements of the sheet cause the thread to move up or down, and cause the needle to turn. The needle moves the broom straw pointer.

Your homemade barometer, if carefully built, will be fairly sensitive to changes in air pressure. If it goes dead after a few days, that may be because the plastic or rubber sheet is not quite airtight (some kinds leak air very slowly) or because you didn't do a really airtight job in fastening it to the side of the can. In any case, don't expect to see violent motions of the pointer—an approaching front may move the pointer one-eighth of an inch to one-half of an inch in a day.

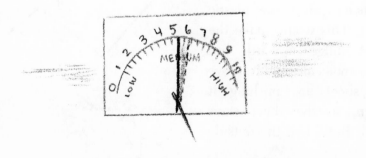

Examining the Air

One way to test your barometer is to take it for a ride in an elevator. As you ride up, the air pressure decreases (because there is less air above you) and the needle should slowly move toward lower numbers. How far it moves depends on the tightness and thickness of the sheet, and how far up you take it. The barometer sketched in this chapter showed a half-inch movement of the broom straw during a ten-story ride.

This type of barometer has one disadvantage—it feels changes in the *temperature* of the air as well as in the pressure. When the air in the can becomes warmer, the molecules bounce faster and push harder; when the air becomes cooler, they bounce more slowly and push with less force. For the most accurate results, then, keep your barometer in a place where the temperature changes as little as possible—a closet or a cellar, for example. If possible, take your readings at the same time every day.

In taking a reading, the important thing to look for is the *change* in air pressure. Rising pressure usually means increasingly cool, heavy air; falling pressure means increasingly warm, light air.

If you have seen a commercial barometer, you may have wondered about the words, STORMY, RAIN, CHANGE, FAIR, DRY, VERY DRY, on the dial. You can ignore them, for they mean very little. The position of the pointer doesn't tell the story. What matters is whether the pointer is moving toward higher or lower pressure.

That's why you can't tell anything about the coming weather just by looking once at the barometer. You have to look at it, make a note of the pressure, and then look at it again several hours later or the following day. Then you can tell whether the pressure is rising or falling, whether the approaching air mass is cold and heavy, or warm and light.

AIR MOVEMENT INDICATOR

This is not a weather instrument, but an easy-to-build gadget that shows which way the air is moving. With it you can trace the air currents in your room as they rise, spread across, descend, and return.

MATERIALS NEEDED

A drinking straw, a piece of paper about 3 inches wide and 4 inches long, 2 paper clips, a pencil, a pin, an empty spool, and scotch tape.

HOW TO BUILD IT

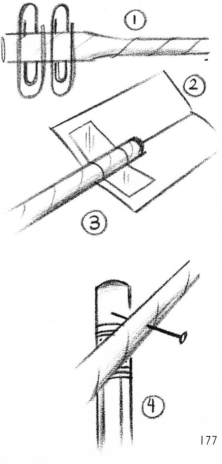

Flatten out 1 inch of one end of the straw and slide two paper clips on this end.

Now gently crease the paper down the center the long way. Open up the fold and lay the paper flat on the table.

Hold the straw so that the clips are straight up and down. With scotch tape, fasten about one inch of the other end of the straw into the crease of the paper.

Push a pin into the center of the straw and into the eraser of the pencil. Wiggle the straw a little so that it can turn easily on the pin.

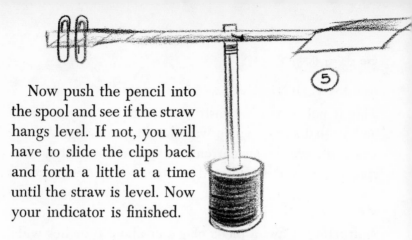

Now push the pencil into the spool and see if the straw hangs level. If not, you will have to slide the clips back and forth a little at a time until the straw is level. Now your indicator is finished.

Hold it over a warm radiator or lighted lamp and you will see the paper rise. Hold it directly under a refrigerator door and open the door an inch or two, and you'll see the paper go down. Now you know which way shows warm rising air and which way shows cold descending air. Carry it around the room to trace the flow of air.

Chart for Weather Observations

Date	Time	Barometer reading	↑→↓	Temp.	Humidity	Rain	Wind direction	Speed	Sky	Forecast

Notes on use of this chart.
  Try to take your readings at about the same time every day.
  The arrow symbols refer to rising, steady, and falling air pressure.
  In the sky column, use these symbols: ○ clear, ◑ partly cloudy, ● cloudy.
  The sky column can also be used to record the type of clouds seen.

EYES AND NOSE ON THE WEATHER

You can forecast the weather in all kinds of ways. Your homemade weather bureau can give you some advance information, and so can the daily weather map. But there are other ways too. People have found that a change in the weather announces itself by many signs that can be understood without the use of instruments or maps. A look at the sky, a sniff of the air, even the behavior of a bug can sometimes give you a hint of the weather's coming attractions.

WEATHER SIGNS IN THE SKY

Dark clouds in the west—
Stay indoors and rest.

Anyway, don't plan on outdoor fun, because there's a fair chance of rain or snow coming your way. A good deal of the weather comes from the west, so when you see dark clouds there, the likelihood is that they are coming your way. Their darkness shows that they are thickly loaded with tiny raindrops. Just a bit of cooling can make them cluster into larger drops, heavy enough to fall and spoil your plans.

When the sunset is clear,
A cool night draws near.

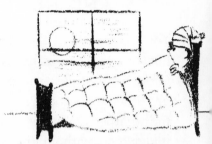

Clouds act as a sort of mirror that reflects heat. When there are no clouds in the sky, the earth's heat can escape after the sun sets, and the night will be cool—or at least cooler than if there are clouds that keep the heat from escaping.

When high clouds and low clouds do not march
together,
Prepare for a blow and a change in the weather.

Clouds move in different directions because the winds blow them that way. The approach of a front is usually signaled by winds that shift and change, with the lower and upper winds moving in different directions. With a front comes a change in the weather.

> *When clouds move down and turn dark gray,*
> *A rainy spell is on the way.*

Sounds like a warm front, doesn't it? The clouds "go downstairs" as the slanting front moves toward you, until finally the low, gray nimbostratus clouds are over you and the steady rain begins.

> *A ring around the sun or moon*
> *Brings rain or snow upon you soon.*

The ring is caused by tiny ice crystals high in the air. These scatter the sunlight or moonlight in the form of a ring. The ice crystals show the high-up tip of a warm front coming your way. When the lower portion reaches you, you'll probably be treated to rain or snow.

WEATHER SIGNS IN AND AROUND YOUR HOME

When radio programs are peppered with static,
There'll be lightning and thunder and weather
aquatic.

The crackling sound of static is caused by radio waves—not the ones sent out by radio stations, but by lightning flashes. When you hear static without seeing lightning, it's because the lightning is zipping around some distance away or within the clouds themselves. In any case, there is a fairly good chance that a thunderstorm will follow shortly.

When windows won't open and salt clogs the shaker,
The weather will favor the umbrella-maker.

Sticky windows and damp salt are signs of very humid air, with some likelihood of rain on the way.

Smoke drifting lazily, close to the ground,
Tells us that rain may be coming around.

Warm, damp air has less pressure than cool, dry air. Having less pressure, it is less able to push up the smoke, which just drifts along without rising. Of course, warm, damp air doesn't always mean that rain is coming, but there is a fairly good chance that it will.

Welcome the sound of crackling hair—
It tells of weather clear and fair.

When you comb your hair, you scrape electrons from your hair onto the comb. When a great many electrons have piled up, they jump back to your hair, and that's the crackling sound you hear. Dry air makes a poor pathway for electrons, so that quite a large number of them must pile up before they have enough push to jump across to your hair. When they jump, they make a good-sized noise. But moist air makes a good pathway, so that the electrons keep streaming back in tiny clumps, too small to make a noise.

Of course, crackling hair simply means that the air *right around you* is dry. If you happen to be combing your hair in a heated room, the air may be quite dry even though it is raining outside. And if your hair is damp, you won't hear any crackles even on a very dry day. But otherwise the rule holds true; hair crackles in dry air, and dry air means clear weather.

When teeth and bones and bunions ache,
Expect the clouds to fill the lake.

You have probably heard people say, "It's going to rain. I feel it in my bones." Often it turns out that way too, often enough to have made scientists look into the matter. They think that it may be a matter of blood

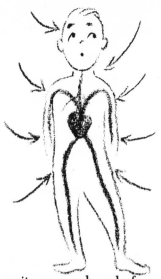

pressure and air pressure. Your blood is under pressure because it is being constantly squeezed and pumped by your heart. This blood pressure would make you swell up slightly, but the pressure of air against you prevents it. When the air pressure becomes weaker, it can't push against your blood pressure quite as much as before, so it may be that a tiny amount of swelling actually takes place. You don't ordinarily feel it, but perhaps some people have sensitive spots in their bones, skin, or teeth that make them aware of the change in air pressure. So, when warm, moist, low-pressure air comes along before a rain, they complain of aches and pains.

WEATHER SIGNS FROM PLANTS AND ANIMALS

Hark to the cricket, whose chattering sound
Will tell you how hot is the air near the ground.

Some people claim that you can tell the temperature of the air by counting the chirps of a cricket. Try it yourself, if you happen to be within earshot of a cricket. Count the number of chirps in 15 seconds, add 37, and the answer should be the temperature. Of course, you'll also need a thermometer to check your result.

Flies and mosquitoes are biting and humming;
The swallows fly low; a rainstorm is coming.

Some scientists think that insects fly low in damp air because their wings become damp and heavy. If this is so, you can see why you would hear them buzzing around you before a rain, and why they would stop to rest more often, clinging to any convenient support, including you.

As for the swallows, they are insect-eaters that catch their meals on the wing. When the insects fly low, so do the hungry swallows.

When marshy smells and flowery perfumes
Invade the air, a rainstorm looms.

Again it seems to be a matter of air pressure. Before a rain, the air pressure is weaker; it presses less strongly against things. With less air pressure squeezing against them, flowers are more able to send out perfumed vapors that make the air fragrant. Unfortunately, the same weakened air pressure also releases less pleasant odors from decaying plants in marshes.

Through long experience, farmers know these signs. That is why they sometimes say, "It smells like rain."

There are thousands of little sayings about the weather. Every part of the country has its own special little sayings, and so does every other part of the world. Workers in almost every trade and profession have their own special beliefs about the weather. Some are true, and others are nothing but superstitions that have long since been proven false.

Every day the weather scientists learn more and more about what makes the weather. Every day their forecasts become more accurate. But there is a great deal more to find out. In the meantime, you can still have the fun of finding out for yourself. But as you watch today's weather and attempt to forecast tomorrow's, here's something to keep in mind:

> *In spite of how the flowers smell,*
> *And what the birds and bees can tell,*
> *And whether bones and bunions swell,*
> > *Your forecast can be wrong,*
> > *So very very wrong!*
> *In spite of the barometer,*
> *The rain gauge and hygrometer,*
> *Also the anemometer,*
> > *You still can be so wrong,*
> > *So very very wrong!*

INDEX